OSPREY COMBAT AIRCRAFT • 52

US NAVY F-14 TOMCAT
UNITS OF OPERATION
IRAQI FREEDOM

SERIES EDITOR: TONY HOLMES

OSPREY COMBAT AIRCRAFT • 52

US NAVY F-14 TOMCAT UNITS OF OPERATION *IRAQI FREEDOM*

TONY HOLMES

OSPREY
PUBLISHING

Front cover
On 10 April 2003, Lt Cdrs Jeff Ohman and Mike Peterson were tasked with performing a Forward Air Control (Airborne) (FAC(A)) mission in central Baghdad in VF-2's F-14D Tomcat 'Bullet 100' (BuNo 163894). The aircraft's pilot, Lt Cdr Ohman, later recalled;

'We launched off USS *Constellation* (CV-64) in the cover of darkness and proceeded to our area of responsibility. Once having completed our inflight refuelling, we checked in with the controller for tasking. There was a beautiful sunrise that morning as we approached Baghdad. As the FAC(A) crew on scene, we were capable of coordinating multiple assets in support of the ground commander's intent. Most of the time, we were the airborne eyes of the battlefield, enhancing the situational awareness of the ground-based troops. We could guide them to avoid areas of conflict when possible.

'The Marines had already pushed into the city, concentrating on the military infrastructure of the country along the way. Every once in a while, they would meet with pockets of resistance. That is what occurred on the morning of the 10th. While pressing through central Baghdad with a tank and some Humvees, the Marines noticed that they were taking fire. We were able to help them locate from which direction the rounds were coming, as well as the general area, so that they could focus their attention on eliminating the threat.

'The two USAF A-10s that were on-station overhead were used as the low attack/gun strafing assets to keep the aggressors' heads down. This enabled the ground troops to take up a better firing position. An artillery battery was also used to provide suppressing fire, coordinating its shelling with the attacks being made by the airborne assets on scene. Amongst the latter were two RAF Tornado GR 4s, which used their Enhanced Paveway II laser-guided bombs (LGBs) to disable the aggressors, while Army Blackhawk helicopters employed their door-mounted guns in between bombing strikes in an effort to suppress enemy small arms fire.

'Once the resistance was surgically disabled, without inflicting any casualties on nearby civilians, the ground element was cleared to continue its progression into central Baghdad. With our assistance no longer required, we returned to a nearby tanker to top off our fuel. From there, we checked out with the overall airspace controller and returned to the carrier'. (*Cover artwork by Mark Postlethwaite*)

First published in Great Britain in 2005 by Osprey Publishing
Midland House, West Way, Botley, Oxford, OX2 0PH

ISBN 1 84176 803 0

Page design by Tony Truscott
Cover Artwork by Mark Postlethwaite
Aircraft Profiles by Jim Laurier
Index by Alan Thatcher
Origination by Grasmere Digital Imaging, Leeds, UK
Printed in China through Bookbuilders

05 06 07 08 09   10 9 8 7 6 5 4 3 2 1

EDITOR'S NOTE
To make this best-selling series as authoritative as possible, the Editor would be interested in hearing from any individual who may have relevant photographs, documentation or first-hand experiences relating to the world's elite pilots, and their aircraft, of the various theatres of war. Any material used will be credited to its original source. Please write to Tony Holmes via e-mail at:
tony.holmes@osprey-jets.freeserve.co.uk
or
tonyholmes67@yahoo.co.uk

CONTENTS

INTRODUCTION

The Tomcat's contribution to the winning of Operation *Desert Storm* in 1991 was, by any measure, minimal. Despite more than 100 F-14s being committed to the campaign, the ten units that saw combat in the war proved more useful in the photo-reconnaissance mission than in the aircraft's primary fighter role. However, the same could not be said about the five units that went to war in Operation *Iraqi Freedom* (OIF) 12 years later. Tomcat pilots and radar intercept officers flew myriad missions in their 52 jets, performing air defence, precision bombing, forward air controlling (airborne) and photo-reconnaissance missions across Iraq.

This volume focuses on the Tomcat's final large-scale campaign with the US Navy in a career that stretches back 30 years. OIF was a huge success for the F-14 squadrons committed to the action, as this book reveals.

ACKNOWLEDGEMENTS

A significant number of naval aviators who flew the Tomcat into combat from the decks of US aircraft carriers in OIF have made a contribution to this book, and the finished volume is considerably better for their valued input. Access to the men and women of the US armed forces who are currently engaged in the War on Terror has tightened up considerably in the post-9/11 world that we now live in. However, thanks to the personnel who man the US Navy's Chief of Naval Information (CHINFO) News Desk in the Pentagon, I was able to meet and interview key Tomcat aircrew soon after their return home from OIF. I would like to take this opportunity to thank CHINFO's Cdr John Fleming, Lt Cdr Danny Hernandez and Lt(jg) David Luckett for handling my request so swiftly, and COMNAVAIRLANT's Deputy Public Affairs Officer Mike Maus and NAS Lemoore's Public Affairs Officer Dennis McGrath for providing me with base escorts 'in the field'.

Thank you also to my old friend and naval aviation historian Cdr Peter Mersky, whose constructive criticism of the text and generous hospitality were most welcome in equal measure. I also owe a great debt to Lt Cdr Mike Peterson (a Tomcat veteran of OSW, OEF and OIF), who diligently read through the manuscript to ensure its accuracy from the end-user's perspective – he also contributed several fascinating combat accounts for the book. Thanks also to PH3 Todd Frantom, who supplied examples of his CVW-5 OIF imagery, PH2 Dan McLain for his VF-2 stills, and Christopher J Madden, Director Navy Visual News Service. Photographers Dave Brown, Richard Siudak, Cpl Gary Dixon RAAF, Ginno Yukihisa, Troy Quigley, Erik Lenten and Erik Sleutelberg also made important contributions. Timely information was provided by Capts Steve Millikin and Jan Jacobs of the Tailhook Association, Capt Zip Rausa of the Association of Naval Aviation, Cdr Dave Baranek, Lt Col Mark Hasara, Maj Dave Glover (of VMFA(AW)-533), David Isby, Gary Sheehan and Bob Sanchez.

Finally, thank you to the following pilots and naval flight officers (NFOs) from the following units whose OIF experiences, and photographs, are featured in this volume;

CVW-2 – Capt Mark Fox, Capt Craig Geron, Capt Larry Burt and Lt Cdr Dave Grogan
CVW-8 – Capt David Newland
CVW-14 – Lt Cdr Jim Muse
VF-2 – Cdr Doug Denneny, Cdr Dave Burnham, Lt Cdr Jeffrey Ohman, Lt Cdr Mike Peterson, Lt Sean Mathieson and Lt(jg) Pat Baker
VF-31 – Cdr Rick LaBranche
VF-32 – Cdr Marcus Hitchcock, Cdr Russell Ariza, Lt Cdr David Dorn, Lt Tim Henry and Lt(jg) Dave Dequeljoe

VS-38 – Lt Cdr Carlos Sardiello
VFA-83 – Lt Cdr Matt Pothier
VF-103 – Lt(jg) Matt Koop
VF-154 – Cdr Douglas Waters
VF-213 – Cdr John Hefti, Lt Cdr Marc Hudson, Lt Cdr Larry Sidbury and Lt(jg) Kenneth Hockycko

Tony Holmes, Sevenoaks, Kent, March 2005

OSW

'I want to congratulate each and every one of you for your performance in Operation *Iraqi Freedom*. You are demonstrating for all the world to see that the United States has the greatest naval air power in the history of the world. Hostilities are still in progress, but Iraq has been liberated. Our president and country called upon you for your courage, dedication and skill. You responded with precise, persistent combat air power. We have seven aircraft carriers and air wings deployed in response to OIF. Each aircraft carrier is a sovereign piece of American territory – collectively, the most potent striking force ever assembled, and in working jointly with our allies, a remarkable testimony to our flexibility and capability'.

This statement, released to the Naval Air Force by Vice Admiral Mike Malone, Commander Naval Air Forces Pacific, in June 2003, effectively sums up just what the US Navy brought to OIF. Naval aviators flew more than 1000 sorties in the opening stages of the conflict, and by mid April 2003, this figure had exceeded 6500 from aircraft carriers in-theatre. No less than 64 per cent of these had been strike and close air support (CAS) missions. All of this was achieved with the commitment of one fewer aircraft carrier/air wing – USS *Nimitz* (CVN-68) and CVW-11 arrived in the Northern Arabian Gulf (NAG) right at the end of the war – than in Operation *Desert Storm* in 1991.

Strictly adhering to the current US Navy mantra of 'quality, not quantity', the effectiveness of the aircraft sent into combat in 2003 more than made up for any shortfall in numbers in comparison with the force sent to help free Kuwait 12 years earlier.

The employment of smart weapons such as the Joint Direct Attack Munition (JDAM), Joint Stand-Off Weapon (JSOW) and new-generation laser-guided bombs (LGBs), combined with better tactics and more versatile aircraft, allowed the Navy to make an greater contribution to 'Gulf War II' in comparison with its efforts in *Desert Storm*.

Tailhook extended, and carrying a TARPS pod on station five and two AIM-9Ms on the shoulder pylons for self-protection, VF-31's F-14D BuNo 164600 breaks into the recovery pattern overhead CVN-72 at the end of yet another OSW photo-reconnaissance mission in early 2003. The fifth from last Tomcat ever built, this particular aircraft was delivered to the Navy by Grumman on 31 March 1992. It was initially used to train new Tomcat pilots and RIOs with West Coast F-14 Fleet Replacement Squadron VF-124 at NAS Miramar, California, and was passed on to VF-101 Det Miramar (also known as 'Det West') following the disbandment of the former unit in September 1994. Transferred to VF-31 in early 1997, BuNo 164600 flew as 'Tomcatter 104' until re-marked as the unit's CAG jet, featuring all-black fins, in November of that same year. In late 2000 the aircraft became the CO's mount, complete with VF-31's traditional red twin fins and a gloss black radome. A veteran of three *WestPac* deployments, and flown hard during CVW-14's ten-month OEF/OSW/OIF cruise of 2002-03, BuNo 164600 was scheduled for a major overhaul upon its return to Oceana. However, due to the Tomcat's impending retirement, it was decided that the money involved in refurbishing the jet could be better spent elsewhere. BuNo 164600 was duly stricken on 16 June 2003 and categorised as fit only for SARDIP (Stricken Aircraft Reclamation and Disposal) at the Norfolk Naval Aviation Depot on base at Oceana (*Lt Cdr Jim Muse*)

Driven by the USAF's outstanding use of smart bombs dropped from multi-role aircraft such as the F-15E and F-16A/C during the latter conflict, the Navy invested significant sums of money in the 1990s on technologies that ultimately ensured 'one weapon, one target destroyed'.

Desert Storm veteran Rear Admiral Pat Walsh, Commander Carrier Strike Group Fourteen and former boss of Carrier Air Wing One, explained why the Navy was forced to change the way it went to war;

'In the Cold War blue water Navy, we taught ourselves to work autonomously. This was because we did not expect to have allies fighting alongside us in any conflict with the Soviet Union. We expected to use their infrastructure and their bases, but we never dreamed that they would take up arms and fight alongside us. The real lesson the Navy learned in the 1991 conflict with Iraq was what you can do when you work with an ally, whether it be in the joint ranks or the Coalition ranks. We had not put together architecture prior to that which would allow us to become more effective in our unilateral operations. Prior to 1991, we worked pretty much autonomously in the Arabian Gulf.'

The Navy's carrier-based weaponry and systems also reflected its Cold War mentality, and naval aviators such as Rear Admiral Walsh were caught by surprise when they watched the imagery being shown to them on television screens aboard ship;

'Like all naval aviators involved in *Desert Storm*, I was astounded by the TV pictures released by the USAF of precision munitions striking targets. We had nothing like this in the fleet. Part of our problem in this area was in the way we traditionally evaluated our mission success. Our strike aircraft were bereft of the equipment that allowed such vivid imagery of bombs hitting targets to be brought back to the ship in real time for post-mission analysis. We had to rely on a dedicated reconnaissance platform for this imagery – F-14s carrying TARPS (Tactical Aerial Reconnaissance Pod System) in *Desert Storm*. The Tomcat could not capture imagery of bombs actually hitting targets as was the case with the USAF's laser-guided smart bombs. We had no way of conducting "real-time" bomb hit/bomb damage assessment.'

Although a valuable reconnaissance platform, the aircraft which proved to be the most ineffective during *Desert Storm* as a direct result of the Navy's Cold War strategies was the iconic F-14 Tomcat. Built exclusively as a fighter interceptor, and tasked with repelling waves of missile-carrying Soviet bombers hell bent on sinking US Navy carriers, the ten Tomcat units that were sent into action had to resign themselves to predominantly flying combat air patrols over the NAG, hundreds of miles south of the real action in Iraq. And with the Iraqi Air Force's reluctance to attack naval ships, the F-14 crews saw little fighter action.

Tomcats were kept out of the action because the Navy had failed to develop the necessary systems and procedures required to integrate carrier air groups as part of a joint air component command. This meant that F-14 crews were unable to solve the strict rules of engagement (ROE) that would have allowed them to autonomously engage aerial targets using only their onboard sensors. Instead, they relied on controlling platforms such as USAF E-3 AWACS aircraft to give them their clearance to fire

With the ROE criteria met, fighters with Beyond Visual Range air-to-air missiles like the AIM-7 Sparrow and AIM-54 Phoenix could fire their ordnance at long range, safe in the knowledge that no friendly aircraft in the area would be shot down instead. USAF F-15 pilots could solve all the required ROE criteria for identifying an enemy aircraft from within their own cockpits, prior to shooting it down. The F-14, conversely, lacked the systems and software to meet all ROE criteria, which left its crews reliant on outside clearance to engage. The job of defeating the Iraqi Air Force was therefore given to the Eagle pilots, who duly shot down 35 aircraft.

Inter-service rivalries also played a big part in the F-15's success in *Desert Storm* according to a veteran Tomcat RIO interviewed by the Author. He stated that 'there was lot of parochialism as to where the F-14 and F-15 CAPs were placed. The Eagles got the kills because it was the USAF's E-3 AWACS that were running the show up north. They would even call Navy guys off and then bring in Eagles for easy pickings. This could just be the ranting and raving of pissed-off Navy pilots, but from what I personally saw in OIF, there was a shred of truth in these stories'.

The post-*Desert Storm* years were bleak ones for the Navy's fighter community, with swingeing budget cuts seeing ten frontline Tomcat units decommissioned due to the jet's limited mission capability and astronomical flight-hour costs. Yet just when it looked like the F-14's ocean-going days were numbered, a reprieve came thanks to the accelerated demise of another Grumman 'Ironworks' product. The all-weather, long-range A-6 Intruder bomber was hastily taken out of service, again due to high maintenance costs and the supposed evaporation of its mission in the post-Cold War world.

With the Intruder on the verge of retirement, and the Tomcat seemingly following in its footsteps, the Navy now found itself facing a shortage of tactical carrier aircraft to fulfil its global 'policing' mission.

When the F-14 was developed in the late 1960s, Grumman had built the jet with the capability to drop bombs, although this mission requirement had not been specified by the Navy. For the first 20 years of its fleet life, the Tomcat had been operated exclusively as a fighter, with the photo-reconnaissance role introduced in the early 1980s. Threatened by wholesale decommissioning, the fighter community looked to diversify in order to survive, and seeing that the all-weather precision bombing role once performed by the A-6 was now vacant, a push was made to pair the F-14 up with some form of bolt-on targeting pod.

Experimentation with gravity bombs hung beneath standard Tomcats had taken place as early as November 1987, although senior naval officers realised that the F-14 would not be a viable fighter/attack platform without a precision weapons delivery capability. Little funding was available to develop an all-new system for the Tomcat, so an 'off-the-shelf' targeting pod was acquired thanks to the securing of modest financing through the lobbying of Commander Naval Air Forces Atlantic in the autumn of 1994. The equipment chosen was the combat-proven AAQ-14 LANTIRN (Low Altitude Navigation and Targeting InfraRed for Night) pod, developed for the F-15E by Martin Marietta.

Working with a tiny budget, the Tomcat community, ably assisted by a clutch of defence contractors, integrated the digital pod with the analogue F-14A/B, and by March 1995 a test aircraft – supplied by VF-103 – was dropping LGBs with the aid of LANTIRN. The results of this early evaluation were stunning, with the Tomcat crew obtaining better infra-red imagery, and bomb accuracy, than the similarly-equipped USAF F-15E and F-16C . On 14 June 1996, the first fleet-capable LANTIRN pod was delivered to VF-103 at NAS Oceana. During the ceremony held to mark this occasion, Secretary of the Navy John H Dalton proudly proclaimed 'The Cat is back'.

To give an unsophisticated bomber like the F-14 a precision targeting capability, the basic LANTIRN system was modified into the US Navy-specific LTS (LANTIRN Targeting System) configuration. The LTS removed the navigation pod of the two-pod LANTIRN system and vastly improved the targeting pod for Tomcat use. The Navy pod featured an embedded GPS and inertial measurement unit that provided the pod line-of-site cueing and weapon release ballistics. The RIO had a much larger display in his cockpit than the one presented to his equivalent Weapon Systems Officer in USAF aircraft, which led to better apparent magnification and target recognition.

Unlike its USAF configurations, the LTS performed all the weapon release calculations and presented release cues that it had generated to the aircrew. It also incorporated a masking avoidance curve display and, eventually, a north orientation cue and 40,000 ft-capable laser. The latter was extremely useful in allowing F-14 aircrew to employ LGBs above potential threat system altitudes, and it came into its own in the higher terrain of Afghanistan during Operation *Enduring Freedom* (OEF).

As a pseudo-reconnaissance asset, the LTS generated coordinates for any target located on the FLIR. A later software modification known as T3 (Tomcat Tactical Targeting) increased the accuracy of the coordinates produced by the LTS, and allowed for the first rudimentary TACAIR onboard generation of coordinates suitable for GPS guided weapon (JDAM, JSOW and CBU-103 WCMD) employment. The first combat use of this capability was in OEF, when a T3 LTS-equipped Tomcat generated coordinates for a B-52 that dropped CBU-103 WCMD (wind-corrected munitions dispenser, which was basically a GPS-guided Rockeye cluster bomb) from over 40,000 ft. These weapons duly scored direct hits on a vehicle convoy that had stopped after the initial truck had been destroyed by the Tomcat with LGBs.

But all that lay in the future, for in June 1996 the F-14/LTS partnership remained unproven in combat. Nine months earlier, in a pre-cursor of things to come, the Tomcat briefly had the chance to prove its worth in the 'mud moving' business when, on 5 September 1995, during Operation *Allied Force*, two F-14As from VF-41, embarked in USS *Nimitz* (CVN-68), dropped LGBs (designated by F/A-18s) on an ammunition dump in eastern Bosnia.

OSW

Aside from brief campaigns in the Balkans and Afghanistan, combat operations for F-14 crews have

The Lockheed Martin AN/AAQ-25 LANTIRN Targeting System (LTS) pod is always carried on station 8B, this piece of equipment being exclusively responsible for revolutionising the F-14's combat employment in the jet's final decade of frontline service with the US Navy. Featuring an integral GPS for position information and an inertial measurement unit for improved stabilisation and accuracy, the pod also boasts an internal computer with ballistics data for the various precision munitions carried by the F-14. Data is fed to the pod by the Tomcat's AWG-9 (F-14A), AWG-15 (F-14B) or AN/APG-71 (F-14D) radar, but the LTS in turn only sends video and guidance symbology to the crew's cockpit displays. This meant that few wiring and software changes had to be made to the Tomcat in order to allow it to operate the LTS. All pod controls are in the RIO's cockpit, although the bomb release 'pickle button' is situated up front with the pilot. The LTS cost the Navy around US$3 million apiece, and due to its high cost only 75 were bought for fleet use. Typically, a squadron would take six to eight pods with it on deployment, and these would be permanently fitted to the non-TARPS jets. This particular pod is fitted to an F-14D of VF-2, embarked in CV-64 in late 2002 (*PH2 Dan McLain*)

taken place almost exclusively in the NAG since *Desert Storm*. In the wake of this conflict, a No-Fly Zone was created over southern Iraq, and for 12 years Navy Tomcat crews policed these areas. The first of these zones was established in the aftermath of *Desert Storm* in an effort to offer protection to the Kurdish population in northern Iraq from President Saddam Hussein's forces. Initially covering all Iraqi airspace north of the 36th parallel as part of Operation *Provide Comfort*, the legality of this mission was mandated by United Nations Security Council Resolution 688.

When the Shi'ite Muslims also began to suffer persecution in the south, a No-Fly Zone was created with UN backing as Operation *Southern Watch* (OSW) on 26 August 1992. Joint Task Force-Southwest Asia (JTF-SWA), consisting of units from the United States, Britain, France and Saudi Arabia, was established on the same date to oversee the running of OSW. Like the operation in the north, which was officially titled Operation *Northern Watch* (ONW) on 1 January 1997, OSW saw US, British and French aircraft enforcing the Security Council mandate that prevented the Iraqis from flying military aircraft or helicopters below the 32nd parallel – this was increased to the 33rd parallel in September 1996.

The US Navy's principal contribution to OSW was the mighty carrier battle group, controlled by Fifth Fleet (which had been formed in July 1995) as part of the unified US Central Command (CENTCOM), which oversaw operations in the region. Typically, an aircraft carrier would be on station in the NAG at all times, vessels spending around three to four months of a standard six-month deployment committed to OSW. Ships from both the Atlantic and Pacific fleets took it in turns to 'stand the watch', sharing the policing duties in the No-Fly Zone with USAF and RAF assets ashore at bases in Saudi Arabia, Kuwait, Bahrain and other allied countries in the region.

OSW's original brief was to deter the repression of the Kurdish and Shi'ite populations through the imposition of a No-Fly Zone, but it soon became obvious to the Coalition that the Iraqi Army was more than capable of dealing with the disruptive elements in both the north and the south without having to involve the Air Force. Frustrated by its inability to defend the people it had encouraged to rise up and overthrow Saddam's regime in 1991, the US-led Coalition subtly changed the emphasis of its ONW/OSW mission. This saw the systematic monitoring of Iraqi military activity in the area evolve from being a useful secondary mission tasking to the primary role of the crews conducting these sorties from the mid 1990s.

By December 1998, the justification put forward by the US government for the continuation of ONW/OSW was the protection of Iraq's neighbours from any potential aggression, and to ensure the admission, and safety, of UN weapons inspectors.

The Tomcat proved to be a primary asset in OSW, although not because of its ability as a long-range fighter. As had been the case in *Desert Storm*, the F-14's TARPS capability provided JTF-SWA with the flexibility to monitor Iraqi military activity on a daily basis in good weather. Although the TARPS mission was seen as a necessary evil by a number of dyed-in-the-wool fighter crews, it nevertheless enabled the Tomcat community to make a concrete contribution to the daily enforcing of OSW. The TARPS missions also tended to be far more eventful than the typically mundane and boring Combat Air Patrols that were the 'bread and butter' sorties of the F-14 units in the NAG in the years prior to the arrival of LTS-equipped aircraft.

Seasoned Tomcat crews would also be quick to point out that the absence of the Iraqi Air Force in the No-Fly Zone for over a decade was proof positive that the many thousands of CAP missions flown in that time achieved the desired result from JTF/SWA's point of view.

The actualities of a typical No-Fly Zone mission did not alter much throughout the duration of OSW, with most following a set pattern as follows. Thanks to the established routine of the operation, and the advent of secure e-mail communication between JTF-SWA's Combined Air Operations Center (CAOC) and the air wing aboard the carrier in the NAG, shipboard mission planners would usually get a rough outline of the Air Tasking Order (ATO) 'frag' (tasking) about 72 hours before it was due to be flown. As each day passed, more information would be relayed to the ship to the point where, 24 hours before the package was due to launch, its participants had a detailed plan of where they were going and what they were doing, as well as the role being played by other supporting assets sortied from shore bases.

On the day of the mission, assigned crews (five Tomcats would be committed to the evolution, with four actually flying the mission and the fifth launching as the airborne spare) would start their OSW briefing about two-and-a-half hours prior to take-off. This was an air wing-wide meeting that was usually attended by every single person launching on the mission. This lasted for 30-45 minutes, after which F-14 crews would return to their own squadron ready room and conduct the division brief applicable to their part in the mission – this ran for 15 minutes. Crews then broke up into sections to conduct individual briefs, where they would discuss things like in-flight emergencies and what to do during the sortie from a single aircraft standpoint. This process would effectively see the participating units go from 'back row', to 'mid-level' to 'micro view'.

One of the air wing's biggest advantages when compared with shore-based OSW assets was that all mission elements briefed together, face-to-face. Air wings would do this on a near-daily basis when on cruise, talking at length about various mission profiles and operational developments. This also allowed the Navy to run bigger packages into Iraq. USAF groups, on the other hand, all briefed separately, and then met up to support each other inbound to the 'Box', as the southern No-Fly Zone was dubbed by Coalition aircrew.

Tomcat crews would go 'feet on the deck' to their jets 45 minutes prior to launch, by which time the aircraft was fully fuelled, all systems (bar the engines) were up and running thanks to the jet's auxiliary power unit and the pylon-mounted weapons, or TARPS pod, had been secured.

This TARPS image, taken by the crew of a VF-2 jet in early 2003, is typical of the photo-reconnaissance material that was captured by the Tomcats in the NAG during the 12 long years that the OSW mission was performed by US carrier battle groups. Here, a series of command and control bunkers have been knocked out by three JDAM dropped from F/A-18Cs assigned to CVW-2. This kind of BHA material was crucial for the CAOC when it came to assessing the effectiveness of the Iraqi air defences in the lead up to OIF (*via VF-2*)

The jet was then preflighted at deck level for 10-15 minutes, after which the Radar Intercept Officer (RIO) would climb aboard and commence his radar systems and avionics checks. With 30 minutes to run to launch, the air wing's Air Boss (who runs the flight deck) would call 'starts away', and the aircraft were fired up. With everything functioning as it should be, the five Tomcats would be unchained and marshalled in a pre-ordained order to one of the ship's four catapults for launching.

Having successfully departed the carrier, the pilot would find the duty tanker using the aircraft's radar in air-to-air search mode, rather than 'breaking comms' by talking on the primary control frequency known as Strike in order to get a steer from an AWACS controller. Having located the tanker, he would join the line of aircraft formating off its left wing, waiting his turn to cycle through and 'top off' the Tomcat's capacious tanks. With the refuelling complete, the pilot positioned the jet back in the formation, but this time off the tanker's right wing.

The air spare would return to the carrier at this point if all four of the primary aircraft had tanked successfully and all the mission-crucial systems – weapons, radio, radar homing and warning receivers and avionics – were functioning correctly.

Most strike groups were then divided into two mini packages once on station so as to cover any Periods of Vulnerability (known simply as vul time to naval aviators). This tasking was easier to perform when dealing with smaller divisions of aircraft, rather than sending in a huge formation of jets that tended to get in each others' way. The first group, including a section of Tomcats operating exclusively as fighters (pre-1997), fighter-bombers or in the TARPS role, would commence its vul time, leaving the second package on station for a short while longer, prior to it too being committed. There was a small period of overlap between the two packages as a result of this tactic being employed.

Each package had a designated vul time in the 'Box' according to the ATO, and each of these slots had been meticulously worked out by JTF-SWA's CAOC. This organisation, based in Saudi Arabia, was responsible for all No-Fly Zone mission planning, and it created a daily ATO for Coalition participants (both naval and shore-based aviation assets)

It was standard operational procedure that if the package did not make it into southern Iraq during its set time slot, the jets would not be allowed 'over the beach'. Once in the 'Box', the jets pressed on along pre-planned routes until arriving on their designated patrol station in south-eastern Iraq. Crews remained in constant contact with one of four Air Traffic Control agencies while performing an OSW mission. One of these would be in a combat information centre aboard a US Navy AEGIS class cruiser in the NAG, another in a purpose-built radar control centre in Kuwait near the Iraqi border, a third in the 'big wing' tanker that was on station supporting the package and the fourth in an orbiting E-2 or E-3 AWACS. These controllers kept all TACAIR elements in the 'Box' updated on what the Iraqis defences were doing in response to the mission.

Thanks to the Tomcat's immense range, it was not uncommon for F-14 sections to double cycle during OSW missions. Both jets would stay inside the 'Box' for the entirety of the sortie, while the Hornet section it had ingressed with remained on station for as long as the jets' fuel permitted, before being replaced by two more F/A-18s. The Tomcats would finally depart with the second section when the pilots of the latter aircraft declared that they needed fuel. This effectively meant that the F-14s had stayed on station for twice as long as the Hornets, and all on a single tank of fuel.

With the mission completed, the Tomcats would go 'feet wet' back over the NAG and head south along pre-planned routes to a tanker. The latter would be either a USAF KC-10 or KC-135, a RAF VC10 or Tristar or two 'organic' S-3 Vikings that had sortied with the strike package from the carrier and then stayed on station over the NAG, awaiting their return. Cycling through the refuelling procedure once again, topping off their tanks at about 500 lbs above what was needed to land back aboard the ship, the aircraft would overfly the carrier, proceed back into marshal and then wait their turn to recover. A typical OSW mission usually lasted around four hours, depending on whether or not a target was bombed during the course of the patrol.

OSW HIGHLIGHTS

Following a series of widespread Coalition air strikes on targets in southern Iraq in January 1993 (with naval assets provided by CVW-15, embarked in USS *Kitty Hawk* (CV-63)), subsequent OSW operations in the 'Box' passed off largely without incident for the next five years. Throughout this period, F-14 units assigned the TARPS mission diligently photographed vast tracts of southern Iraq in order to monitor troop movements and locate AAA and SAM sites.

Having escorted strike aircraft in the NAG since 1991, Tomcat crews were finally given the chance to drop bombs on targets in Iraq in the early hours of 16 December 1998 with the launching of Operation *Desert Fox*. A four-day aerial offensive ostensibly aimed at curbing Iraq's ability to produce Weapons of Mass Destruction (WMD), this campaign was also triggered by Saddam's unwillingness to cooperate with UN inspections of known weapons sites. Many observers believed that the primary aim of *Desert Fox* was to attack the Iraqi leadership in a series of decapitation strikes. To this end, a presidential palace south of Baghdad was hit, as

Having coming out of the 'Box' for mid-cycle gas, the crew of VF-31's 'Tomcatter 101' await their turn on the hose while the pilot of VFA-25 F/A-18C BuNo 164635 tops off his tanks with fuel from an RAF Tristar K 1 of No 216 Sqn in February 2003. The latter jet was flying from Muharraq, Bahrain, where it had also been based during Operation *Desert Storm*. The RAF usually has at least one Tristar or VC10K permanently deployed in Bahrain, supporting Coalition jets venturing into Iraq. Big wing tankers were in great demand in both OSW and OIF, and as CVW-2's Lt Cdr Dave Grogan explained to the Author, the Tristar was a particular favourite of US Navy TACAIR pilots;

'We would take fuel off of anyone who had it available in-theatre – USAF, Navy, RAF or RAAF. I personally preferred to tank from a British L-1011 TriStar rather than a USAF KC-135 or KC-10, as the basket in the Lockheed jet was a lot easier on our probes than its USAF equivalent. The RAF jet's lighting system was also a much easier to work with at night'
(*Lt Cdr Jim Muse*)

were buildings that housed the Special Security Organisation and the Special Republican Guard.

In the vanguard of these precision strikes on the first night of the operation were the F-14Bs of VF-32, flying from USS *Enterprise* (CVN-65). Part of a 33-aircraft force launched by CVW-3, the Tomcats headed into Iraq in the wake of concentrated Tomahawk missile attacks. *Desert Fox* was an all-Navy show on the 16th, as described by an a F-14 strike leader from VF-32;

The ten F-14Bs of VF-32 were in the vanguard of the precision strikes flown by CVW-3 from CVN-65 in December 1998 as part of Operation *Desert Fox*. Here, a squadron maintainer carefully applies LGB silhouettes to the fuselage of his assigned aircraft, thus denoting the ordnance dropped by this particular jet (BuNo 161870, which subsequently participated in OIF II with VF-143 in 2004). The Tomcat/LTS partnership proved to be spectacularly successful during the four-day campaign (*PHAN Jacob Hollingsworth*)

'The first night was all Navy, NO Air Force – not even their tankers – or Brits. It was designed for a single cycle so as to achieve the element of surprise. Our F-14s were loaded with two 1000-lb GBU-16 LGBs, and our target was within Baghdad city limits. Tomcats were assigned most of the hard targets because of the aircraft's LTS capability – collateral damage was unacceptable. We found our targets and "schwacked" them. To watch those buildings go away through the LTS cockpit display was impressive. We were opposed by ballistic-launched SAMs and AAA.'

On the last night of *Desert Fox* (19 December), CVW-3 strikers were joined by aircraft from CVW-11, embarked in USS *Carl Vinson* (CVN-70) – the latter carrier had only entered the NAG eight hours earlier. At the heart of the CVW-11 strike force were LTS-equipped F-14Ds of VF-213, employing LGBs with deadly accuracy and lasing targets for the trio of Hornet units assigned to the air wing.

By the time *Desert Fox* had come to an end, CVW-3 and CVW-11 had flown more than 400 sorties in the 25+ strikes launched during the campaign. VF-32 alone had dropped 111,054 lbs of ordnance, consisting of 16 GBU-10s, 16 GBU-16s and no fewer than 26 2000-lb GBU-24 penetrator LGBs. The latter proved to be the weapon of choice against hardened aircraft shelters, HQ bunkers and command and control buildings. Not all of the Tomcats sortied were carrying bombs, however, as both VF-32 and VF-213 conducted a series of escort CAPs for USAF B-1Bs committed to *Desert Fox* from day two of the campaign.

Although the operation had lasted just four days, its consequences were felt right up until OIF in March 2003. Proclaiming a victory after UN weapons inspectors had left Iraq on the eve of the bombing campaign, and stating that he no longer recognised the legitimacy of the No-Fly Zones, Saddam brazenly challenged patrolling ONW/OSW aircraft by moving mobile SAM batteries and AAA weapons into the exclusion zones. Both were used in the coming months, and Iraqi combat aircraft also started to push more regularly into the 'Box'.

The adoption of this more aggressive stance by the Iraqi Air Force almost resulted in a US Navy Tomcat claiming its first Phoenix missile kill when, on 5 January 1999, two F-14Ds from VF-213 fired two AIM-54Cs at MiG-25s that had penetrated the No-Fly Zone. The Iraqi jets had already turned back north and were making a high speed run for

home by the time the Tomcats got to fire their missiles at very long range. Neither hit their targets.

Iraq's open defiance to OSW meant that Coalition aircraft patrolling in the 'Box' were now regularly locked up by fire-control radar and engaged by AAA and unguided SAMs on a near-daily basis. In the post-*Desert Fox* world, these violations provoked a swift, but measured, response from JTF-SWA. Typically, reliatory missions – dubbed Response Options (ROs) – were devised within the CAOC-approved pre-planned strike framework. ROs allowed No-Fly Zone enforcers to react to threats or incursions in a coordinated manner through the execution of agreed strikes against pre-determined targets such as SAM/AAA sites and command and control nodes.

On 9 September 1999, following significant opposition to recent patrols, CVW-2, embarked in USS *Constellation* (CV-64), launched Operation *Gun Smoke*. Some 35 of 39 AAA and SAM sites targeted for destruction in the 'Box' were eliminated in a series of precision strikes that saw the largest expenditure of ordnance in a single day since *Desert Storm*. The F-14Ds of VF-2 played a leading role in this campaign, and aside from dropping LGBs and lasing for AGM-65s fired from F/A-18s, the unit also got to fire a single AIM-54C at long range against an Iraqi MiG-23. Again, no hit was registered.

During the first nine months of 1999, US and British aircraft had flown 10,000 OSW sorties and dropped 1000 bombs on 400 targets. This level of action was sustained into the new millennium, and between March 2000 and March 2001, Coalition aircraft were engaged more than 500 times by SAMs and AAA while flying a further 10,000 sorties into Iraqi airspace. In response to this aggression, which had seen Coalition aircraft fired on 60 times since 1 January 2001, US and British strike aircraft dropped bombs on 38 occasions.

Below
The crew of VF-2's GBU16-toting F-14D BuNo 164351 prepare to strap into their jet during the Operation *Gun Smoke* on 9 September 1999. This 24-hour OSW offensive saw CVW-2, embarked in CV-64, expend the most ordnance in a single day since *Desert Storm*. VF-2 led the air wing by destroying 35 of the 39 targets assigned – S-60 (57 mm) and KS-19 (100 mm) AAA pieces and surface-to-air missile sites – around Basra. OIF veteran Capt Larry Burt was CO of CVW-2's VFA-137 during *Gun Smoke*, and he recalled;
'VF-2 crews would attack a AAA site with their own LGBs, then bring the Hornets in with Laser Mavericks (LMavs). The F-14 guys would find another gun, call in the Hornet, join up on the run-in and lase the target with their LTS. This combination proved deadly, with one F-14 crew destroying ten guns on one mission alone – four with their LGBs and six with LMavs' (*US Navy*)

The most comprehensive of these RO strikes (indeed, the biggest since *Gun Smoke*) occurred on 16 February 2001 when CVW-3, operating from USS *Harry S Truman* (CVN-75), targeted five command, control and communications sites. Again, VF-32 found itself in the vanguard of the one-day war, dropping LGBs, lasing for fellow Hornet strikers, running TARPS missions and conducting Defensive Counter Air (DCA) sweeps in the 'Box'.

The steady escalation of the conflict in the region was only brought

to a halt, albeit temporarily, by the devastating attacks on the World Trade Center and the Pentagon on 11 September 2001. The subsequent declaration of the War on Terror by President George W Bush saw carrier battle groups under Fifth Fleet control removed from their OSW station and pushed east into the Arabian Sea in order to support OEF in Afghanistan. With much of the aerial firepower in this conflict being provided by carrier aircraft flying long missions over land-locked Afghanistan, OSW sorties by the US Navy were suspended. This allowed the Iraqis to move more air defence weaponry below the 33rd parallel.

By the spring of 2002, the Taleban regime had been removed from power in Afghanistan, and the US government's focus of attention returned once again to its old foe in the region, Saddam Hussein. Proof of this came with the arrival of USS *George Washington* (CVN-73) and its embarked CVW-17 in the NAG in late August 2002, the vessel's assignment to OSW marking the first time a carrier had performed this mission in almost a year. Within days of its arrival, the air wing (including VF-103) was conducting RO strikes after being consistently engaged by AAA and SAM radars during patrols over southern Iraq.

The adoption of ROs as the primary means of enforcing OSW evolved to match the Coalition's desire to ensure the safety of its crews flying over Iraqi territory. Initially, the near-immediate air strike response to SAFIREs (surface-to-air fires, involving AAA or SAMs) that had been the norm before and immediately after *Desert Fox* was replaced with delayed, punitive strikes that were usually flown the same day as the No-Fly Zone violation took place. This RO evolved post-9/11 into an even more considered approach, whereby the Coalition adopted the policy of attacking any Iraqi military target in the southern No-Fly Zone. It did not even have to be the one that prompted the reaction in the first place. This, in turn, led to the adoption of the pre-planned RO methodology in the final months of OSW as the battlefield for OIF was prepped.

Having already spent two months conducting OEF missions over Afghanistan, CVW-17's spell in the NAG was to last just three weeks. CVN-73 then headed back into the Mediterranean, and Sixth Fleet control, before returning home in December. By then its place in the NAG had been taken by USS *Abraham Lincoln* (CVN-72), which was in the early stages of a marathon ten-and-a-half-month cruise. Like CVN-73, the vessel had supported OEF prior to its push into the NAG in late October 2002, although the crews of the embarked CVW-14 had not seen action during their long patrols over Afghanistan.

This was all set to change once they commenced OSW thanks to the Bush administration's focus on presenting the case for war against Iraq due to its alleged development and stockpiling of weapons of mass destruction. Links between Saddam's regime and Osama Bin Laden's al-Qaeda network were also played up, and the end result of all this talk was the decision, in September 2002, by US Defence Secretary Donald Rumsfeld to step up the level of response to Iraqi threats to US and British jets conducting OSW sorties. Full-scale conflict was now inevitable.

JDAM TO THE FORE

A key weapon in the revised RO for OSW was the Joint Direct Attack Munition (JDAM), which became CAOC's 'bomb of choice' post-OEF thanks to it being fully autonomous after release, unlike laser-guided or electro-optical munitions, whose accuracy can be affected by bad weather or poor targeting solutions. A clinically accurate weapon against fixed targets, which proliferated in OSW, JDAM is effectively a standard Mk 83 (1000-lb), BLU-110 (1000-lb, penetrator), Mk 84 (2000-lb) or BLU-109 (2000-lb, penetrator) unguided bomb fitted with a GPS guidance control unit (GCU), mid-body ventral strakes and a tail unit that has steerable control fins.

Developed by precision weapons pioneer Boeing in the mid to late 1990s, the JDAM differs from other GPS-guided weapons (AGM-130 and EGBU-15) in that it guides completely autonomously after being released. It cannot be steered or fed updated targeting data once dropped.

The 'baseline' JDAM is considered to be a 'near precision' weapon, the bomb's GCU relying on a three-axis Inertial Navigation System (INS) and a GPS receiver to provide its pre-planned or in-flight targeting capability. The INS is a back-up system should the GPS lose satellite reception or be jammed.

With GPS guidance at its heart, the JDAM can only be employed by an aircraft fitted with an on-board GPS system so that GPS-computed coordinates can be downloaded to the weapon for both the target itself and the weapon release point. That way the jet's onboard INS remains as accurate as possible while the weapon is acquiring a GPS signal after being released. This effectively means that the jet has to have a MIL-STD 1760 databus and compatible pylon wiring in order to programme the bomb's aim point, intended trajectory shape and impact geometry.

Achieving initial operational capability in 1997, JDAM made its frontline debut during the NATO-led bombing campaign in Serbia and Kosovo during Operation *Allied Force* in 1999. It was then progressively employed during OSW, primarily by the US Navy, until the weapon really began to capture headlines during OEF thanks to the exploits of Navy Hornet units operating from the various carriers assigned to the conflict. JDAM finally made its combat debut with the Tomcat (2000-lb GBU-32V(2) version only, carried exclusively by the F-14B) in February 2002, again in OEF, and on the eve of OIF with the F-14D – the A-model Tomcat could not employ JDAM because it lacked a digital databus.

Aside from its stunning accuracy in OEF, the weapon also proved popular with crews because it could be released in level flight from high altitude, thus allowing aircraft to stay above any SAM or AAA threats. Depending on the height and speed of the delivery platform, JDAM can be released up to 15 miles away from its target in ideal conditions.

Following several embarrassing targeting failures of LGBs in OSW in the autumn of 2002, including one which almost severed an oil pipeline, CAOC began to favour the employment of JDAM weaponry almost

A 2000-lb GBU-31(V)2/B JDAM is attached to the bomb pallet beneath the fuselage of a VF-2 F-14D on the eve of OIF. Although this weapon proved effective in the 'Shock and Awe' phase of OIF, its post-war use has been somewhat limited due to its size, as VF-2 RIO Lt Cdr Mike Peterson explained;

'The 2000-lb JDAM is a great way to level a building, but that is not always the desired effect. As Mk 80 series bombs increase in weight, the percentage of explosive goes up greatly. A 2000-lb Mk 84 (2039 lbs in weight, of which 945 lbs is explosive) is about 2.5 times as powerful as a 1000 lb Mk 83/BLU-110 (1014 lbs in weight, of which 385 lbs is explosive) and five times as powerful as a 500-lb Mk 82 (500 lbs in weight, of which 192 lbs is explosive). Collateral damage re-emerged as a more significant factor after the end of major hostilities, and the 2000-lb JDAM was not deemed suitable for most targets.'

For OIF II/III, F-14s have been armed with GBU-12 LGBs, as VF-103's Lt(jg) Matt Koop recalled;

'We were JDAM capable and did lots of training on it in work-ups, but the decision was made that for maximum flexibility (Maxflex) we would have our Hornet wingman carry a 500-lb GBU-38 JDAM and one other bomb – usually a GBU-12, but later they started carrying a LMav. We used GBU-12s the entire time. Maxflex was the name of the game, since we mostly encountered "pop up" targets without mensurated coordinates. GBU-12s also minimised collateral damage'

The first unit to take the LTS pod on deployment back in 1996, VF-103 was also the first Tomcat unit to benefit from the more aggressive RO policy instigated in OSW post-OEF. However, some poor LGB work in the 'Box' in early September 2002 by a CAG staff RIO flying with the unit almost resulted in the severing of an Iraqi oil pipeline north of Basra, and the CAOC immediately banned any further bombing by F-14s in-theatre. Prior to being reassigned to OSW, VF-103 had spent two months supporting Coalition forces in Afghanistan by flying CAS, FAC(A) and TARPS missions from the deck of USS *George Washington* (CVN-73). After just three weeks in the NAG, the carrier chopped out of Fifth Fleet control and sailed into the Mediterranean Sea to operate with Sixth Fleet for the rest of its deployment. These F-14Bs are seen on a training mission over the NAG in September 2002, the aircraft nearest to the camera (BuNo 163221) being configured for TARPS, as it lacks the LTS pod carried by the lead jet (BuNo 161422) (*Capt Dana Potts*)

exclusively. This continued up until the final battlefield prepping in early March 2003.

Restricted to carrying LGBs only, the F-14D units committed to the final stages of OSW felt more than a little frustrated at being cut out of the action due to their lack of JDAM compatibility. There was also a feeling within the Tomcat community that the USAF-dominated CAOC was using this as an excuse to keep the choice RO missions for land-based units preparing for OIF. One senior naval aviator serving with VF-2, which arrived in the NAG with CVW-2 aboard CV-64 on 17 December 2002 as relief for CVN-72, recalled;

'We felt that the Air Force-led CAOC was saving the best targets for USAF assets, few of whom had JDAM capability in any case. Navy crews believed there was some consternation within the Air Force that a carrier-based aircraft such as the F-14 could conduct deep strike missions into western Iraq against high value targets that the USAF was determined to save for itself, and its aviators. This left us Tomcat crews feeling like the bastard children of the OSW Coalition.

'I experienced this at first hand right from the start of our time on station in the NAG. On 26 December 2002, CVW-2's Hornets conducted a big strike with JDAM near An Nasiriyah in retaliation for the shooting down of a Predator UAV (unmanned aerial vehicle) four days earlier. We really wished we could have dropped too, but there was no trust in-theatre for Tomcats with LGBs – JDAM was now the name of the game. This was very frustrating because the CAOC would allow USAF aircraft to drop LGBs, but they wouldn't let us.

'We were pretty sure this was because CVW-17's VF-103 was the last Tomcat unit in-theatre to be cleared to drop LGBs. They were tasked with conducting a handful of ROs, and during one such mission a senior aviator in the air wing bungled his LGB delivery and sent the bomb wildly off target, nearly severing a major oil pipeline. The unit had blown it big time. The CAOC therefore couldn't and wouldn't trust the Tomcats to deliver LGBs until the very last days of OSW. This was a painful lesson, and Tomcat aircrew were very upset at their comrades from Oceana putting a "turd in the punchbowl" for everyone that followed. It was very, very frustrating to be over the targets and not be able to employ our LGBs.

'A typically fruitless OSW sortie for VF-2 at the time went as follows. Almost always flying at night, and using Night Vision Goggles (NVGs), we would launch with our weapons (usually two LGBs), refuel from USAF tankers, check in with a myriad of control agencies, do a roll call at the beginning of a vul window and then press out and perform either our Strike Familiarisation, TARPS or DCA missions. We would then usually go back to Kuwait (the southern part) and get mid cycle gas.

'Sometimes an RO was called away. Routinely, the AWACS controllers would read out the call-signs of the guys they wanted to be "droppers" and then switch them up to another radio frequency over which they would relay specific targeting information. The unwanted jets – usually F-14s from VF-2 – were then told to return to the carrier. Not being given a mission to perform was like being picked last in football. The Hornets were doing great work with JDAMS, while we were left to act as high-speed cheerleaders.

'During this period, I had even been the overall strike lead for the CVW-2 jets in the "Box" when the USAF controllers came on the radio and called my guys away to do their thing. We would simply turn around and go home, later slapping the Hornet guys on the back when we saw them at the mission debriefing in CVIC (carrier intelligence centre). Although it was nice to see "my strike" get the job done, especially after the hours and hours that I had put into the mission with pre-flight planning, it would have been far more rewarding had we been "cleared hot" to attack the target too. This lack of trust of the Tomcat and its LGBs motivated the VF-2 aircrew to push the system to release new software that would allow the F-14Ds to drop JDAM.'

The crucial piece of equipment required by VF-2 to allow it to employ JDAM was the D04 mission tape, which enabled the F-14D's databus to communicate with GPS-guided ordnance. VF-2's XO for much of the unit's 2002-03 OSW/OIF cruise was veteran Tomcat RIO Cdr Doug Denneny, and he explained that the unit had lobbied hard for D04 to be made available prior to CVW-2 deploying;

'When VF-2 set sail for the NAG on 2 November 2002, we were well prepared for potential combat operations. Our ten F-14Ds were in excellent condition, our morale was high and we were pretty confident that our timing was going to be good for what we considered was a foregone conclusion that we would invade Iraq.

'The biggest disapointment prior to deployment was that our aircraft were not yet configured with the new computer software upgrade referred to as D04. The latter gave the F-14D many excellent upgraded capabilities, including compatibility with the GBU-31V(2) JDAM. We pushed very hard during work-ups to have the testing of D04 completed in time for the upgrade to be installed in our jets. Unfortunately, the test community and NAVAIR were around two years behind schedule on the tape, and in mid-2002, while we were in the final stages of work-ups, they found further problems with the tape which caused still more delays. Our chain of command and my CO (Cdr Andrew Whitson) and I were not interested in taking an immature tape on cruise, so we left without what we considered to be an incredibly important war-fighting tool.

'Once we arrived in the NAG, we quickly realised just how important JDAM had become to the overall prosecution of OSW. We could also see that our participation in the early phases of any fully blown conflict would be jeopardised without D04. VF-2 began pushing for the tape's accelerated release, despite the reluctance of certain senior leaders in the deployed air wings, and throughout the Navy as a whole, to have the tape installed in our F-14Ds in time for combat.

'As in most bureaucracies, the more senior you get, the more risk adverse you become – this was definitely the case with D04. Unquestionably, their reticence was grounded in many sea stories with the perils of bringing immature systems into the operator's hands, and then having the operators hurt themselves, or someone else, due to anomalies in a software load. However, we were convinced to back the tape by ex-Weapon School instructors Lt Cdrs Keith Kimberly and Mike Peterson, now serving with VF-2, who had been intimately involved with the development of D04. They knew more about the tape than just about anyone else in the Navy, and they knew that the F-14D units needed it.

'Thanks to some backroom lobbying by Tomcat proponents in the Pentagon, the senior leadership in the Navy was informed that the remaining tape testing could be rapidly completed through the immediate release of funding allocated for future expenditure on D04 in the months to come. Upon receiving this news, the Vice Chief of Naval Operations directed NAVAIR to spend the money immediately and get the tape out to the fleet. VX-9 and the F-14 Software Support team at Naval Air Warfare Center (NAWC) China Lake worked hard to complete the final bomb drops in record time – all flight testing had been completed within 30 hours of the request being received!

'A rapid action response team was then assembled from personnel within NAVAIR, VX-9 and NAWC, and they were sent to the three deployed carriers operating F-14Ds in order to install the D04 tapes.'

By the time the D04 team arrived in-theatre, four of the five carriers to be committed to OIF had arrived on station either in the NAG or in the eastern Mediterranean. And it was in the latter region that the ten Tomcats of VF-213, serving with CVW-8 aboard USS *Theodore Roosevelt* (CVN-71) became the first F-14Ds to be upgraded with D04 from 12 February 2003. The team then headed south to the NAG.

VF-2 was the next unit to receive the upgrade, after which the D04 team shifted its attention to the ten F-14Ds of VF-31, which had returned to the NAG with CVN-72 in early February 2003. Having ended its OSW commitment in December and then made it as far east as Perth, Western Australia, on its way home, the *Lincoln* battle group was instructed to turn around and head back to the NAG to help bolster the Coalition forces massing in the region.

Although VF-31 was the last squadron to receive the D04 upgrade, this had some benefits for the unit, as CVW-14 staff officer Lt Cdr Jim Muse (who regularly flew with the unit as a RIO) explained;

'Although the squadron had less time to learn the new system, the NAVAIR engineers that were installing the tapes knew exactly what they were doing by the time they got to us. When they had modified the VF-213 aircraft, they had found that there were some interface issues between the tape and the jets' mission computers, but a quick-fix modification was put in place and the conversion timetable got back on track. Guys from both VX-9 and the Weapons Test Center also helped

Above
VF-2's F-14D BuNo 159613 takes on fuel from a KC-10 during a pre-war DCA patrol in the 'Box' in late February 2003. CVW-2 relied heavily on tanker support in OSW and OIF, as staff pilot Lt Cdr Dave Grogan explained;

'The biggest limiting factor to the generation of sorties in OSW/OIF from a naval aviation perspective was the availability of airborne gas in-theatre. We faced an extra challenge flying from "Connie", as CV-64 was positioned furthest south of all three carriers in the NAG. We were always tight on fuel, and in order to avoid running out, you had to be very efficient when it came to getting to the tanker for mid cycle gas both two and from the target (*PH2 Dan McLain*)

out, bringing their upgrade kits with them. By the time they got to VF-31, they had the modification pretty much down pat.

'When the team came to us on *Lincoln*, they brought two fully functioning mission computers with them, which allowed the conversion of our aircraft to be accomplished very quickly. This was just as well, for in order for the engineers to upload the D04 software into the jet they had to modify the aircraft's databus – the latter was a no turning back mod, which changed the databus for good. If anything had gone wrong with the upgrade, VF-31 may well have been ruled out of OIF.'

All three F-14D-equipped units in-theatre were keen to prove the jet's new precision bombing capabilities in combat prior to the campaign commencing, and on the night of 28 February 2003 VF-2 got the chance to do just that. Flying the first F-14D to drop a JDAM in anger was prospective squadron executive officer Cdr Dave Burnham;

'I was leading a section in the "Box" when my RIO, Lt Justin Hsu, and I were instructed by our AWACS controller to carry out a RO strike on a military intelligence facility in Basra. This gave us the chance to use JDAM, which we had only been carrying in live form for the previous 72 hours. There was very little in the way of AAA opposing us that night, and I don't remember seeing anything exploding at our altitude – that may have been because I was so focused on not screwing up with this new weapon! We simply drove into the target area and hit the bomb release when the symbology cue appeared in the HUD. Afterwards, my RIO and I spoke about how anti-climactic the whole event was. We were both in agreement that the creators of JDAM had really taken the skill out of

CVW-14 was lucky enough to make two visits to the US Navy's favourite R&R port during its marathon *WestPac* in 2002-03, CVN-72 initially spending Christmas at anchor off Fremantle, Western Australia. The vessel duly departed on 28 December 2002 for the final leg home (it was due back in Everett Navy Yard on 20 January 2003), but less than a week later *Lincoln* was told to return to Western Australia for a two-week spell of flightdeck resurfacing off Fremantle in preparation for OIF. The vessel dropped anchor in Gage Roads on 6 January 2003, by which time CVW-14 had sent 20 aircraft ashore to nearby RAAF base Pearce to conduct crew continuation training. Here, three of the four Tomcats flown ashore are seen sandwiched between an E-2C and two EA-6Bs. VF-31 flew bombing missions from Pearce, before flying back aboard ship when the carrier headed for the NAG on 20 January (*Cpl Gary Dixon*)

Opposite left
Its LGBs still on their racks, 'Bullet 111' returns to CV-64 at the end of yet another fruitless OSW patrol in January 2003. The LGB-equipped F-14 was not the preferred CAOC weapon on choice at the time (*VF-2*)

dropping a bomb, as you did not even have to see the target in order to score a direct hit.

'The weather was good that night, so we got our own Bomb Hit Assessment footage of the weapon impacting the target through our LTS. There were other assets in the area filming this drop too, and satellite imagery showing the building both before and after was also relayed to the ship post-mission. There was much rejoicing following this sortie both aboard ship and in the CAOC, as Fifth Fleet and CENTCOM were anxious to ascertain just how well the F-14D interfaced with JDAM. They needed it to work "straight out of the box", as the Tomcat was to play a major role in "Shock and Awe".'

Although this mission proved that the F-14D could indeed employ JDAM effectively, crews found that the GPS-guided 'wonder weapon' occasionally created more headaches than it solved when working with the CAOC. A RIO from VF-2 recalled;

'We used JDAM to execute several ROs where various targets had been identified – usually by UAVs, due to their ability to stay on-station for a very long time with a low profile. Most of our OSW targets were volatile in nature because they were re-locatable or mobile (radar and communication vans, missile launchers etc.). Once a target was located, it was positively identified by the CAOC and the attack coordinates accurately measured for use with GPS-guided weapons. The Collateral Damage Estimate (CDE) was also performed in the CAOC to ensure that only the target would be damaged and no civilian casualties would be sustained. The RO was then called away.

'One problem that we encountered was that the CAOC took a long time to work through targeting and CDE, and often the target would move. If it did – even only a few hundred metres – the whole process would have to start all over again. Aircrew were not relied upon to identify targets themselves at this time.

'The CAOC loved JDAM because they supplied the identification of the target and the coordinates. It turned the aircraft into a dump truck, with no identification or aircrew guidance required. It basically let the CAOC be the shooter, not the aircrew. Unfortunately, JDAM does not work for moving targets, and requires new coordinates (which could not be generated by most TACAIR aircraft at the time) if the target moves and then stops. We spent a lot of time with LGBs on the aircraft and sensors on targets that we were not allowed to hit, or just dump trucking ordnance around waiting for a target to sit still long enough for the CAOC process to work. It was very frustrating for aircrew.

'Once OIF started, many people up the chain of command just didn't get the fact that JDAM was a great weapon for fixed targets – buildings don't get up and move – but had very limited use for the fluid battlefield when trying to address the mobile and re-locatable target set. For it to be of any use the target had to be stationary, and someone in the air or on the ground needed to provide high quality coordinates. The field-based systems capable of producing these coordinates were not widely available, or used. JDAM was good, however, if support was required on bad weather days, and it did allow the war to continue even if it was less effective against the majority CAS and SCAR (Strike Coordination Armed Reconnaissance) set in comparison with other weapons such as LGBs, Maverick/Hellfire missiles and 20 mm cannon.

'Conversely, we were tasked with hitting buildings with LGBs, and then had to abort strikes due to poor weather between us and the ground when JDAM would have been ideally suited for these targets!'

TARPS

Although JDAM now allowed the Tomcat community to get back into the precision strike business, units had continued to earn their keep throughout their unofficial bombing ban by conducting all-important TARPS missions over the future battlefield. VF-2 NFO Lt Cdr Mike Peterson flew a number of photo-reconnaissance sorties in the final weeks of OSW;

'We generated approximately two TARPS missions every three days during OSW, and ramped up to one mission per day in the month preceding OIF. We did a lot of reconnaissance using our LTS pods and Fast Tactical Imagery (FTI) capability, the latter allowing us to send LTS pictures to ground stations via encrypted UHF link, in addition to our traditional wet film and digital TARPS capability.

'A typical mission had up to 25 target areas planned for coverage. We would send either two TARPS jets or one TARPS and one LTS aircraft, depending on the target set and the environmentals. There was some common wiring and control panel locations for TARPS and LTS, so they were mutually exclusive configurations for the F-14. An aircraft could carry both pods in a ferry configuration but one of the systems would be inoperable. The TARPS/LTS combination was helpful in that the latter aircraft could find the target with the FLIR and direct steering for the TARPS jet to capture the higher resolution footage with the pod's stand-off KS-153 camera. The KS-153 has great resolution, but a very small

Opposite bottom right
For many years, the F-14's most important contribution to OSW was as a photographic-reconnaissance platform thanks to its bolt-on TARPS pod – this one is fitted to an F-14D from VF-2. Secured to rear right Phoenix missile station five, the pod originally boasted two wet film (subsequently replaced by Digital Imaging) cameras and a single infra-red line scanner for low-light/night reconnaissance (removed pre-OIF). Although weighing in at 1760 lbs, the pod imposed few performance penalties on the F-14 other than restricting the carriage of missiles/bombs on the aft tunnel stations. TARPS jets were also LTS prohibited because both systems shared common wiring and control panel locations in the Tomcat. TARPS remained in use with the fleet until late 2004, and in its final years of service there were three main types of pod in use. They were the legacy 'wet' film pod, TARPS DI (digital imaging) pod, which used digital cameras that allowed the shots to be viewed in the cockpit and sent back to the carrier or other Link-16 capable aircraft over encrypted UHF, and TARPS CD (completely digital), fitted with digital cameras that auto-sent the imagery when within range of a receiving station. OIF veteran Lt Cdr Mike Peterson explained how VF-2 selected the jets to be used in this role in 2002-03;

'Not every aircraft in the squadron was TARPS capable, as the jet needed to have had its environmental control system (ECS) modified to allow it to pressurise the pod in flight. Our maintenance personnel were having to work flat out to keep at least six of our ten F-14s airworthy at any one time on cruise, leaving them with little time to perform the ECS mod on all of our jets. We tried not to switch the pods around too much, adhering to the principle "if it ain't broke don't mess with it". We usually had a dedicated TARPS jet and two others identified as "good" TARPS aircraft. If we had to load a pod from scratch, and could secure a deck elevator run to get it from the TARPS shop up to the flightdeck (often the limiting factor), it would take us 1-2 hours – depending on jet location and availability – to fit it to the aircraft' field of view. If the tasked coordinates were inaccurate, you could miss the picture entirely.

'On one particular OSW photo-reconnaissance mission flown just prior to the start of OIF, we launched as a section of TARPS aircraft. Our main tasking was to ingress via the Basra Peninsula and flow up the eastern lines of communication to image various targets. We then flew southwest across several major towns and out through Kuwait to the east. The final targets would be the Abot and Kaaot oil platforms in the NAG.

'The initial flow to the north focused on troop concentrations, and the assessment of their reactions to the presence of the forces massing in Kuwait and the NAG. We wanted to see if troops were massing to provide a focused resistance to the kick off of OIF, or whether they were following the instructions that were dictated to them from the numerous leaflet drops that were made in the area in the preceding weeks. There were instructions printed on these leaflets that allowed us to assess the troops' willingness to comply with our instructions once OIF started. It was a clear day, and we successfully imaged all the targets in the area.

'We then turned southwest to line up our targets in the vicinity of As Samawah and An Nasiriyah. The next photo targets were particularly enjoyable in that they were located within known SAM rings. Sometimes, we had targets within the rings, and on other occasions the targets were the SAMs themselves! We used the TARPS imagery to assess the number of launchers and supporting equipment in the rings, as well as to see what their current configuration and operational capability might have been. We proceeded to "take frames and click ass" as we headed through the SAM rings, paying attention to our radar warning receiver (RWR) and maintaining a visual lookout within the section. With no "spikes" on the RWR, we pressed on toward our remaining targets on the way to Kuwait.

'We would usually have both film and gas remaining as we arrived at the Iraq-Kuwait border, so we typically shot some additional targets of interest that had been "informally requested" by the 1st Marine Expeditionary Force (MEF).

'The competition for reconnaissance assets was intense in-theatre during the pre-war build up of forces. With all the UAVs and manned reconnaissance in the area, you would have thought that everyone would get their requests addressed. The reality was that many requests were dropped during the target nomination process, as assets were assigned to targets at higher levels. During one of our liaison trips into Kuwait to visit V Corps and the 1st MEF in preparation for OIF, we briefed them on our TARPS and FTI capabilities, in addition to our Forward Air Controller FAC(A) plan for ground troop support. Both V Corps and the 1st MEF mentioned that they were having trouble getting reconnaissance assets tasked to support their requirements. Specifically, they wanted reconnaissance footage of selected border crossing sites to determine the potential resistance in these areas, as well as photographic coverage of the Iraqi posture in these areas.

'We mentioned that we flew over these areas on almost every officially tasked reconnaissance mission in-country, as well as and on other LTS-equipped sorties too. They gave us their "hot list" and we set up a back door reconnaissance shop to get them the footage that they requested. We always shot the ATO-assigned targets first, but used any "extra" film to

provide support directly to the Army and Marines outside of the normal channels. We provided this footage as often as we could.

'On the way out of Kuwait during the flight back to the carrier, we went by the two massive oil platforms in the NAG to shoot detailed footage of the Iraqi forces pre-positioned on them, and to get good overall pictures of platforms for pre-assault planning use by Special Operations Forces (SOF).'

Thanks to the close working relationship that VF-2 fostered with forces ashore in the final months of OSW, the unit proved instrumental

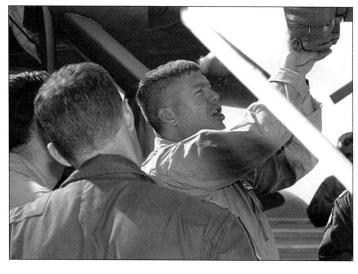

in helping to set up the Kuwaiti Rapid Precision Targeting System (RPTS) station. The squadron also played a part in the integration of RPTS within Coalition Forces Airborne Analysis Cell and Coalition Forces Land Component Command operations. The fixed RPTS station, datalinked with several mobile sites, allowed the sending and receiving of near real time TARPS and FLIR imagery from FTI-equipped F-14Ds of VF-2 and VF-31 patrolling over Iraq.

SHARED WORKLOAD

With the return of *Abraham Lincoln* into the NAG in late January, the OSW mission load was now split between CVW-2 and CVW-14. Staff officers from both air wings immediately set about preparing for the invasion of Iraq as part of OIF, working out how they could best support the Coalition ground assets in their quest to defeat the Iraqi Army. CVW-14's Lt Cdr Jim Muse was intimately involved in this crucial phase of the campaign;

'By the time we arrived back in the NAG, *Constellation* was also on-station, so the workload for OSW was now split between two air wings. However, the CAOC was trying to expand our flight times in the "Box".

VF-2's Lt Cdr Mike Peterson conducts a demonstration preflight of the Swedish-built, dual-purpose Bol LAU-138 weapons rail/countermeasures dispenser system aboard CV-64. Used for the carriage of AIM-9Ms, the rail is filled with 160 rounds of either Bol Chaff or Bol IR. These rails proved hugely beneficial in OIF when the F-14 performed the FAC(A)/CAS mission. F/A-18Cs carried 60 expendables, but with three Bol rails (a normal configuration) and 60 expendables split between the two tail 'buckets', F-14s routinely carried 540 expendables over the beach – a mix of visible flares, low-visible flares, regular chaff, BolChaff, low visibility Bol IR and GEN-X (*PH2 Dan McLain*)

F-14D BuNo 163418 lands back aboard CV-64 following a training mission pre-OIF (*PH2 Dan McLain*)

VF-31's CAG jet in 2002-03 was F-14D BuNo 164601, and it is seen here hook down at the end of an uneventful OSW 'Box' patrol in February 2003. Delivered to the Navy on 17 April 1992, this aircraft also served with Miramar-based VF-124 up until the unit was disbanded in September 1994. Like BuNo 164600 (seen in the photo below), BuNo 164601 then served with VF-101 on both the east and west coasts until transferred to VF-31 in early 2000. The jet duly replaced BuNo 164600 as the 'Tomcatters'' CAG aircraft, and it is set to retain this status until VF-31 retires its F-14Ds in early 2006. BuNo 164601 dropped 19 LGBs and JDAM during OIF (*Lt Cdr Jim Muse*)

'Tomcatter 101' takes on fuel from VFA-115 F/A-18E BuNo 165784, which has been configured as a tanker through the fitment of an Aero D704 Aerial Refueling Store to the jet's SUU-78 centreline pylon. This photograph was taken by RIO Lt Cdr Jim Muse, sat in a second F-14D, during a TARPS mission in early 2003 (*Lt Cdr Jim Muse*)

Previously, the air wing would send a single package of ten to twelve jets into southern Iraq for between an hour-and-a-half and three hours at most, and that would be it for the day. In preparation for war, the CAOC wanted us to significantly expand that footprint so the NAG-based carriers would maintain a near-constant presence in the "Box". That meant launching several complete packages during the time that we were the duty carrier, and it was a lot of flying.

'Rear Admiral John Kelly on *Lincoln* was designated as commander of Carrier Task Force 50 (in charge of all three carriers in the NAG), and a dedicated staff was brought in and assigned the job of deconflicting the flight schedules, alerts, underway replenishments and all the various other details to make sure that one of the carriers was ready to launch jets at any time. CVW-2 on "Connie" apparently volunteered to fly at night, so it switched to nocturnal missions early on in order to get everyone on the correct circadian rhythm. That meant that we were the day boat, and when *Kitty Hawk* showed up, the vessel's CVW-5 generally shared the daylight with us.

'Following CV-63's arrival in the NAG, CENTCOM staged a conference to discuss the problems associated with airspace in the Persian Gulf, and how things would be changed leading up to the big fight. There were jets coming from Qatar, UAE, Diego Garcia and Bahrain, as well as the three carriers in the NAG – literally hundreds of aeroplanes all heading north into Iraq on the first night of the war, and very little space in which to keep them apart. We didn't know if we'd get to use Saudi Arabian airspace at all.

'It was decided that the simplest way to control the airspace was to implement the "driveway" system that had been so effective in OEF. This saw all aircraft using a 15-mile-wide corridor, on which they were deconflicted vertically, laterally and by speed as if on a highway, with jets going north staying on one side and those going south staying on the other.

'It took a while to iron this system out, as we all wanted to use the real layout as soon as possible, but with all of the civilian airliner traffic flying into and out of Kuwait and between Saudi Arabia and Iran, we couldn't fully implement the driveways we wanted to use. CAOC ended up "phasing in" the new scheme, which ultimately meant you never knew for sure if you were using the right one because they were always changing! It drove me nuts because I was working on the "smart packs" for the air wing, and recreating the same "airspace" pages over and over again. I really felt bad for the guys on "Connie" because they were flying at night, and the airspace changes would usually take effect right in the middle of their vul window. It was pretty much a miracle that we didn't have a mid-air over the NAG before or during the war.'

BATTLEFIELD PREPARATION

In the final days before OIF commenced, all three Tomcat units in the NAG (VF-154 had arrived with CVW-5, embarked aboard USS *Kitty Hawk* (CV-63), in late February 2003) were heavily involved in a series of precision strikes against known targets in the 'Box' as part of the battlefield preparation for OIF. CVW-5, which was the designated CAS air wing, hit Republican Guard barracks, HQ and command and control buildings, mobile missile launchers and AAA sites in and around Basra.

On the night of 19 March, assets from CVW-2, -5 and -14, as well as USAF and RAF jets, supported a crucially important long-range mission to H2 and H3 airfields in western Iraq that also involved SOF elements on the ground. One of the VF-2 RIOs involved in this mission gave the following account of the sortie;

'I was in one of two F-14Ds that launched off CV-64 to support a pre-planned operation sent against an airfield in the extreme west of Iraq. By the time it was over, my pilot and I had logged 8.6 hours from launch to trap. Assigned to the mission was a SOF ground element, various TACAIR assets, including sections of A-10s rotating throughout the evening, F-15Es, F-14A/Ds, AWACS and dedicated tankers.

'Our task was to show up after the initial ingress into the area and take over TACAIR asset control in support of the ground element as it headed toward its objective. We started to gain situational awareness of which phase the operation was in as soon as we could get radio contact a few hundred miles out. Having Link-16 JTIDS (Joint Tactical Information Distribution System) was invaluable, as we were receiving datalink to all the other assets in our package without having to use our radio or radar. It sounded like things were going according to plan, and that the assets were getting into position.

'As we got closer, we heard a VF-154 F-14A divert for unknown reasons. We weren't certain if the crew had been engaged by ground fire and been hit, or had some other type of failure, but they had an immediate divert problem and left their wingman on-station to wait for our relief. We quickly arrived on-station and relieved the lone Tomcat as the FAC(A)s for the operation. He passed a turnover brief as he departed, and we started getting a check in from the other assets in the area.

'Our plan was to have at least one Tomcat on station to quarterback the operation, while the other one was headed to or from the tanker – located over the border – to refuel. If required, we would pass control to one of

Below right
This TARPS BHA shot of H2 airfield, in western Iraq, was taken soon after the base had been attacked by Coalition TACAIR assets in mid-March 2003. Nearby H3 was also bombed, and these missions proved to be rather controversial, as a senior naval aviator from VF-2 explained to the Author;

'Before OIF kicked off, the CAOC expressed great interest in striking the early warning "Flat Face" and "Pluto" radars, and their support buildings, sited at H2 and H3 in far southwestern Iraq, near the border with Jordan. Saddam had built this network to listen in on his neighbours to the west, and to defend his country from a surprise attack from Israel. Operating from the designated night carrier, VF-2 was tasked with striking both the radar antennas and the support buildings, as these missions were "fragged" for night only.

'Significant effort was required to get a strike package of F-14Ds off the carrier, refuelled in marginal weather, through 400+ miles of hostile Iraqi skies, over the target and back again. We had to solve challenging time/distance/fuel problems, as there was no way an F/A-18C could make the round trip. And to make matters worse, during those nights in mid-March when we flew these missions, the weather was marginal at best. We were routinely rendezvousing and tanking with USAF tankers over Kuwait in solid cloud, under challenging IFR conditions. After receiving a full top off, the jets pressed out against strong headwinds and began a long transit to duel with the Iraqis, as well as the decision makers in the CAOC.

'Ultimately, the VF-2 jets were never given the clearance to drop their weapons on the radar sites. This was because these missions were viewed as ROs, and therefore governed by OSW rules. For us to receive permission from the CAOC to attack the targets, there had to be a trigger event earlier in the day. These attacks could then be made, even though the antennas were hundreds of miles away from the trigger event. VF-2 crews became increasingly frustrated with these missions. Several memorable "close but no cigar" events happened, one

(continued)

of which involved a section literally counting down the minutes and then seconds left on-station to the AWACS, who would relay this information to the Air Force-led and Air Force-centric CAOC. The F-14 aircrew were led to believe that release authority would be imminent, but they were disappointed once again to have to begin their transit back to the ship.

'Another time, a section of Tomcats flew over the target and then were told to return to the ship because a section of Strike Eagles (who did not have JDAM and could only drop LGBs) were going to be called in to the target instead. The F-15Es were then given clearance to drop. The Tomcat crews were surprised to learn that the Eagles missed wildly, and were even more concerned to observe first-hand the blatant favouritism conducted by the Air Force-led CAOC in handing the mission over to the Strike Eagle crews' *(VF-2)*

the F-15Es if we had both Tomcats off-station. JTIDS was once again invaluable when it came to deconflicting all the assets in our package that were flowing in and out of our Area of Responsibility (AOR) as required, and holding in the same relative area with their lights out. It also allowed us to release the sections on-station when we saw their relief headed inbound without having to constantly query the AWACS as to the status of our support assets. JTIDS provided deconfliction with attacking assets while prosecuting targets on the ground and, most importantly, it let us accurately find the tanker when gas became critical so that we could drive him to us if required.

'Initially, things went pretty smooth for what seemed to be the first 20 minutes, so we headed to the tanker to top off and left our wingman on-station to run the show.

'The tanker was its own unique type of pain this evening. It was WARP (wing aerial refuelling pod) configured, with a boom in the centre. That way it could refuel the USAF assets with the boom or stream the baskets from the wingtips for the Navy jets, which probe refuelled. As we got to the tanker, we joined up on the left side after it streamed the basket. We had to stay pretty well topped off on gas because we would need a significant amount to get to a divert field should we be hit, suffer mechanical difficulties or have a problem refuelling.

'Three things soon became readily apparent as we closed on the tanker;

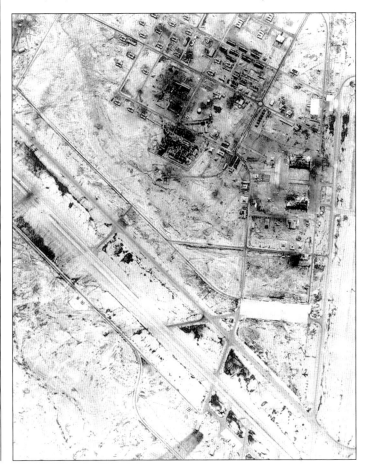

1) we were stuck with manual (unboosted) throttles, so it was like driving a Mack truck without power steering, and therefore very fatiguing on the pilot who was trying to make the minor throttle correction to get in the basket; 2) our probe light, which illuminates the otherwise pitch black basket and lets the pilot see where he's putting the refuelling probe in the endgame, was not working; and 3) there was a lot of turbulence at the tanker's altitude which was causing the wing tips to bounce up and down like a big lumbering bird. This caused the basket to move up and down sporadically about four feet at a shot.

'I stayed on NVGs in the back seat and tried to help talk the pilot into the basket, which was difficult to see without a probe light. Tanking on NVGs was also difficult, as it can seriously distort your depth perception. My pilot got in on the third try, which made us very happy, as the closest divert field was nowhere as close as we wanted it to be.

'As we headed back to the AOR and switched back to the working frequency, things had obviously moved along to the next phase of operations. Our wingman was controlling the engagement of a AAA piece that had started opening up, and we had A-10s and F-15Es attacking vehicles that were moving in the general direction of the SOF units on the ground. We quickly arrived on-station and received control from our wingman as he headed toward the tanker. We were able to take out one of the targets pointed out by the ground element ourselves with an LGB before the dust settled a little bit.

'Now that the initial exchanges had subsided, we gave ourselves about a ten-minute break. The next target that the ground element wanted us to address was located in a revetment about a kilometre away from their present position, but between them and their objective. We had soon located and verified the target with the LTS, and were also able to see the ground unit with our NVGs, but we could not see the target visually with the goggles.

'The release cues from the LTS showed an aim point *after* we were past the ground element position. The SOF team wanted us to illuminate the target with an infrared (IR) pointer to confirm its position before we dropped our LGB on it since it was close to their position. We told them that we couldn't visually put the IR pointer on it because we could not see it through NVGs, but that the LTS indicated that it was clear of their position. After making two passes, and asking for clearance to release, which we did not get because the SOF unit did not acquire us until we were past our release solution, we brought in an F-15E which was fitted with a new Litening II pod. We talked the crew onto the target and verified the ground position with them as well.

'The Litening II-equipped F-15E has an internal IR pointer (unlike our handheld version, which required us to see the target with NVGs), and they illuminated the target that they had located with their FLIR. We saw that the F-15 had the target about 800 metres away from the friendly position, and we passed terminal weapon release control back to the ground element, which in turn authorised the F-15E crew to drop their LGB on their first pass, scoring a direct hit as verified by our LTS. We now headed back to the tanker for round two, as our wingman was on his way back to station.

'The next duel with the tanker took additional tries to get in the basket, and left my pilot with a good cramp in his throttle (left) arm.

'As we arrived back at the fight to join our wingman, the ground unit had reached its objective and was ready to egress the area, which involved moving across a major "enemy line of communication" – a road. We were tasked with sanitising the area where the crossing was to occur, searching out any possible resistance. There were a few vehicles moving along the road, but none were presenting a direct threat to the ground element. We then caught sight of a real fast mover on NVGs doing about 80 mph – easily three times the speed of any other traffic observed, and headed directly for the ground unit. We passed the information to the ground controller, who instructed us to take the vehicle out.

'We rolled in in the same direction that the target was heading and tried to lead it with a LGB, but he was seriously moving. The LGB hit about two vehicle lengths short, but the blast forced the driver off the road. We

This photo was taken by a Tomcat RIO from VF-154 at night through his NVGs, hence the green tinge to the image. His jet is plugged into the basket trailed by a KC-10 somewhere over southern Iraq. Tanking at night was challenging to Tomcat crews even in calm weather, let alone in the turbulent conditions that seemd to proliferate for the duration of OIF. VF-213's Lt Cdr Larry Sidbury was one of those pilots who duelled with the basket on a nightly basis during the war;

'You would wait for the basket to stabilise a little bit before getting plugged in as quickly as you could. You had to be very smooth and gentle on your approach to the basket – you could not afford to make big plays at it. Unfortunately, making unhurried attempts at plugging in did not really sit too well with your ever-dwindling fuel state while flying over hostile territory with nowhere to divert to. The F-14 is a difficult aeroplane to tank, which just compounds your problems. With the F/A-18, when the probe comes out the pilot can see its tip through the HUD, but with the Tomcat, the probe comes out to the side. When I join up, I am having to constantly scan back and forth in order to get lined up correctly. This in turn creates a bow wave off the jet, which moves the basket around. There is a real technique that needs to be mastered when tanking in the F-14'

observed four individuals get out of the vehicle once it had stopped, and they ran into a ditch next to the road. The final person leaving the vehicle had a pretty good heat signature on the FLIR, and he appeared to be severely injured based on the way he rolled into a ditch on the roadside. We watched as the group continued to head away from the damaged vehicle and toward the ground unit. Before we could come back around to see how close the group was getting to the crossing site, an F-15E crew "cleaned up" the scene with their own LGB, and this group was no longer a factor. We covered the rest of the egress by the ground unit, directing other fires as required until we proceeded off-station.

'There was one more trip to the tanker left, and if we topped off, we could make it all the way back to the boat at high altitude on a conservative profile. By the time we got back to the tanker, my pilot was dragging. It was early in the morning hours and still pitch black all around. We had been pumped up during the action, and the flight had been fairly fatiguing. The basket was really bouncing and we were low on gas. We made the decision to take the Tomcat down to the lowest possible fuel state before heading off to the divert airfield (where we could be stuck for days).

'After many attempts, and a severe forearm cramp from running the manual throttles all night, my pilot just steadied about ten feet behind the basket for about a minute. I asked, "Hey, you know we've only got about 400 lbs of gas to play with here before we gotta go?" He replied, "Yeah, I know, but I've got to give it a little break or I'm not gonna make it in".

'With 200 lbs to go (enough for another ten seconds of trying to get in), my pilot made one more attempt and successfully plugged into the basket. The fuel gauge touched the bingo number just as it reversed and started showing good flow from the tanker into our tanks!

'Now we still had the long ride home to end in a Navy specific event – the night trap. En route, we consumed two mocha flavour power bars and a bag of spicy teriyaki beef jerky – a meal that would not be repeated during the war! Once we were feet wet, my pilot levelled with me and said that he was pretty tired – something that a RIO never wants to hear, but I appreciated the honesty.

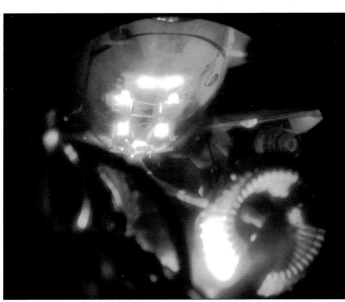

'I implicitly trusted him with my life, and had little worry about his ability to get aboard. It just may have taken us a few tries. I passed him two Red Bulls to see if they would help. He had one right away, and saved the other for closer to the boat – it really did the trick. I don't remember if it was an OK 3 wire, but we were aboard safely on the first pass.'

The next time VF-2 would sortie jets in anger, they would be in the vanguard of the attacks on Baghdad on the opening night of 'Shock and Awe'.

'SHOCK AND AWE'

The Bush administration pre-empted the official start of Operation *Iraqi Freedom* by authorising a daring precision bombing strike on Baghdad on the morning of 20 March. This raid by two F-117s on three homes (also reported as a Republican Guard compound bunker) owned by members of the Iraqi leadership in a suburb on the outskirts of Baghdad had been rapidly generated following a tip-off that Saddam Hussein and four of his top military commanders had been seen entering these buildings. Although the targets were comprehensively destroyed by four EGBU-27 'Have Void' 2000-lb LGBs, the intelligence proved to be incorrect and Saddam remained very much alive.

With OSW now a thing of the past, the three carrier air wings in the NAG and the two in the eastern Mediterranean prepared to undertake the so-called 'Shock and Awe' phase of the campaign. Officially referred to as OPLAN 1003V by Pentagon war planners, this tactical model for the invasion of Iraq had been sold to the US government by senior officers within the Joint Chiefs of Staff as being the best way to ensure that OIF was a swift campaign that inflicted minimal collateral damage on the country's civilian infrastructure.

Rapid domination of the enemy was at the heart of 'Shock and Awe', and military commanders explained to President Bush and Secretary of Defence Donald Rumsfeld that this was only achievable through the mounting of an intense bombardment in the opening days of the war. This would show the Iraqis just how great Coalition firepower was, and prove to them that resistance was useless.

CVW-2's commanding officer, Capt Mark Fox, had been given a high-level briefing in February 2003 on how OIF was originally to be fought;

'The plan called for an air campaign kicked off with a massive air strike ("A-Day", and the beginning of "Shock and Awe"), followed a few days later by the ground war ("G-Day"). The plan evolved, however, as the conflict grew nearer. The gap between "A-" and "G-Days" grew progressively smaller, with good reason – days of heavy air strikes would give the Iraqis the opportunity to sabotage their domestic oilfields and offshore oil platforms before our ground forces could intervene.

'The opening strike – consisting of multiple salvos of cruise missiles and Coalition strike aircraft – targeted hundreds of aim points in several sequential waves, making the first hours of OIF the most overwhelming delivery of precision ordnance ever seen. Designed to saturate and destroy Iraqi air defences, roll back the Baghdad Super Missile Exclusion Zone (SuperMEZ), destroy key command and control nodes and degrade the ground forces' ability to defend Baghdad, the opening strike was pretty impressive for a single evening's work.'

Despite hitting a large number of pre-planned targets on 'A-Day', it appears that the scope of 'Shock and Awe' was deliberately scaled back on the advice of senior military figures in-theatre such as Gen Tommy Franks, Commander of CENTCOM, who was keen to see potential targets such as bridges, water and electricity networks and telephone systems left untouched. This change of tack appears to have come at the eleventh hour, for reports emanating from Washington, D.C. in late January 2003 spoke of a plan to fire some 800 Tomahawk Land Attack Missiles (TLAMs) and Conventional Air-Launched Cruise Missiles (CALCMs) at targets in Baghdad in the first 48 hours of the campaign alone. Manned aircraft would then undertake follow-up strikes against a further 3000 listed targets during this same period.

Instead, CENTCOM's statistics from the war indicate that only about 320 TLAMs (out of a total of 802 for the entire war) were launched on 20/21 March, with the bulk of these preceding the 'A-Day' air strikes on Baghdad on the 21st.

Aside from a small number of CAS missions flown in southern Iraq by CVW-5 and CVW-14, as well as a series of DCA patrols further north, Navy TACAIR assets in the NAG remained unused for the opening 36 hours of OIF until the first 'iron jet' strikes were conducted on Baghdad on the evening of 21 March by CVW-2. Preparation for the 'A-Day' attacks on fixed targets in the Iraqi capital had dominated air wing planning in the lead up to OIF, as Capt Fox recalled;

'In early March, the CAOC assigned Mission Commander responsibilities for the opening strike to CVW-2 based on our schedule. Since the campaign began at night ("H-hour" called for the first bombs to fall on their target at 2100 hrs local), and would be sustained around the clock, we as the night carrier were well situated to conduct flight operations for the first 18 hours of the conflict. And since I was CAG, it was my job to lead the strike. Having spent my entire career in tactical aviation preparing for just this moment, I was in exactly the right place at precisely the right time, and was humbled by the honour.'

VF-2 would play a major part in Capt Fox's 'Shock and Awe' plan for the night of 21 March, with squadron XO, Cdr Doug Denneny, leading the first division of 'iron bombers' over Baghdad;

'I was fortunate enough to participate in the first mission of OIF as a division lead, controlling two Tomcats and two Hornets. My CO was designated as the overall strike lead for an operation scheduled to take place later that day, so as per standard procedure in a frontline squadron, the CO and the XO were assigned separate missions.

'We had been tasked with dropping JDAM on the Ministry of Information's Salman Pak radio relay transmitter facility at Al Hurriyah, southwest of central Baghdad, and in order to effectively employ our ordnance we had to fly into the infamous SuperMEZ which ringed the city. This had become legendary amongst naval aviators during the years of OSW, as the overlapping rings of IADS (Integrated Air Defence Systems) around Baghdad were so dense that they effectively blotted out

With VF-2's XO Cdr Doug Denneny leading the first 'iron jet' strike on Baghdad in the 'Shock and Awe' phase of OIF, it was natural that the CVW-2 brief for the mission would take place in VF-2's ready room. Here, naval aviators from all of the squadrons assigned to the strike study slides of the IADS threat in the SuperMEZ that protected the Iraqi capital. This photograph was taken just hours prior to the 21 March mission. VF-2 RIO Lt Jeff Vallina was one of those who sat in on the brief, and he later recalled;

'This event provided me with one of my most abiding memories of OIF. In the past, during OSW, the Baghdad SuperMEZ had been something that was feared and respected by all Coalition aircrews. The overlapping missile rings were from the Soviet doctrine, and reminiscent of Hanoi and Haiphong during the Vietnam War. Yet, as we were plotting our first night missions over Baghdad, we saw that our flight paths were going straight into the middle of the numerous SAM rings. It was at that moment – more then than when we were actually being fired at over the missile sites – that we as aircrew realised the levity of the situation. All the talk was soon to be over with as the action was about to commence.'

The green-shaded areas on these maps denote the No-Fly Zones in northern and southern Iraq, while the coloured circles illustrate the zonal range for each of the SAM threats in-theatre (VF-2)

Recently brought up from CV-64's hangar deck, 20 GBU-31(V)2/B JDAM sit on their individual Aero-12C skids awaiting dispersion to the Tomcats and Hornets assigned to the opening strikes of 'Shock and Awe' (*PH2 Dan McLain*)

VF-2's Cdr Doug Denneny (left) and Lt Cdr Kurt Frankenberger (right) received DFCs for their mission leadership of the first 'iron bomber' strike on Baghdad in OIF. They are seen here celebrating their 3000th and 2000th Tomcat flight hours (respectively) after a mission over Iraq with the traditional cutting of a cake in the ready room. Both men flew as a crew almost exclusively during the cruise (*VF-2*)

the city itself whenever colour print-outs of the Iraqi capital were produced for threat analysis purposes!

'We had tanked in Saudi Arabia en route to Baghdad, and as we flew over southern Iraq, most of the country was blanketed in a thick undercast layer that stretched all the way up to the Iraqi capital. We were flying the first "iron bombers" to penetrate the SuperMEZ in OIF, and as we headed north, I could see the clouds being illuminated by the explosions of literally hundreds of TLAMs and CALCMs as they struck their targets to signal the start of the "Shock and Awe" phase of OIF. These random bursts of fire looked like lightning strikes in an electrical storm, the cloud cover obscuring my view of the city itself. We were still a long way from Salman Pak, and I nervously watched these explosions taking place for some 30 minutes, fully aware that they were effectively marking our target for us!

'At that stage every explosion I saw was a Coalition weapon hitting its target, rather than any SAMs being fired off in defence of Baghdad. This allayed my fears somewhat, as I found it hard to believe that the IADS threat within the SuperMEZ could survive such a relentless pounding. However, as soon as the explosions stopped – as had been briefed – prior to our arrival, I was alarmed by the sheer volume of AAA and at least a dozen unguided SAMs criss-crossing the night sky ahead of us. The Iraqi gunners and SAM crews had taken a hell of a beating, yet they still seemed to be capable of returning fire the minute our missile attack had ended.

'As we closed on the target I was kept busy dealing with coordination issues for the strike. I had to make go/no go decisions on the attack relative to the weather, which was not good, and our support assets. Our timings began to slip a little too, as our F/A-18 SEAD (Suppression of Enemy Air Defence) section had been delayed en route due to the paucity of tankers – the HARM Hornets showed up so late that we ended up passing them in opposite directions as we headed off the target and they shot their HARMS into the target. We had prioritised them last on the tankers, which is why they were late. Our Prowler support was not in an optimal position either, although they were still able to jam despite their late arrival on-station. Our only dedicated SEAD support was provided by four F-16CJ Wild Weasel aircraft that handled themselves very professionally, unloading HARMS on our ingress. They then left as planned.

'Technically, we were not allowed to enter the SuperMEZ without full SEAD coverage, as the HARMs protected us by hitting active SAM sites on the way in – we had lost some DCA assets en route too. Although we felt pretty naked heading into Baghdad with only the quartet of Wild Weasels to protect us, I made the decision to press on to the target regardless.

'We worked hard to maintain our situational awareness throughout this phase of the mission, keeping our eyes out of the cockpit in order to locate the SAMs and AAA, as well as the remaining members of the division, and all the while jinking, popping flares and pumping chaff. I had the added responsibility of making sure that we were going to hit our release parameters for our JDAM, as the whole reason we were placing ourselves in harm's way was to drop our bombs accurately on the target.'

Piloting Cdr Denneny's F-14 on this mission was VF-2's Administrative Officer, Lt Cdr Kurt Frankenberger. He recalled;

'As we pressed towards the target in what would be a clockwise flow north, then east, then south, we could see the initial TLAM, CALCM and Stealth aircraft weapons impacting in the distance. Our wingman took some great video footage, documenting the target ingress as if he was going to Disneyland – this later made for a nice CNN tape. A medium altitude cloud layer occasionally obscured the lights of Baghdad, but with or without NVGs, the city could be seen getting hit regularly. This was my first combat experience in 17 years of service with the Navy, and my level of anxiety was high.

'As the flight lead of a mixed division of two F-14Ds and two F/A-18Cs, we solved some timing issues and flowed from our Initial Point (IP) on into the target for weapons release. During the 25-mile run from the IP west of Baghdad to the release point, we observed so many SAM launches (10+) that we couldn't count them anymore. Effectively, we had to trust our systems and visually confirm that each missile did not appear to be tracking, then disregard it and evaluate the next one. The more alarming sights were the HARM rounds that were launched from the four F-16CJs behind us. These came out of nowhere and into sight very close to our altitude. You needed to recall the location of the shooter and listen up for the launching calls.

'JDAM delivery went as advertised from our aircraft, although our wingman's jet had a weapons system failure which powered down the JDAM just as he attempted to release his bombs. We kept the speed up for egress and continued to monitor the threat, with constant SAM launches and AAA going off below us to light up the night sky. The explosions

The glow of central Baghdad dominates this shot taken on 21 March 2003 by VF-2 RIO Lt Cdr Will Burney, who captured the image by holding a camera up to one of the tubes of the ANVIS-9 NVGs that he was wearing. Burney, and his pilot Lt Kurt Bohlken, flew as wingmen for Cdr Denneny and Lt Cdr Frankenberger on the 'A-Day' OBS strike package. An extract from Burney's combat account of the mission read as follows;

'Saw a plethora of AAA fire and numerous SAMs as we approached and entered the SuperMEZ, but did not get any RWR (Radar Warning Receiver) indications of anything radar-guided. We had an SMS/MC (Stores Management System/ Mission Computer) failure, which powered down the JDAMs right at "pickle" depression, leaving us with two hung bombs. Dash-1 dropped successfully, and although the clouds precluded FLIR BHA, two flashes through the clouds gave a "warm and fuzzy" that at least the weapons went high order. Had to jettison one of our bombs over the Gulf so that the jet would not exceed our maximum trap weight back at the ship' (VF-2)

VF-2's CO, Cdr Andrew Whitson (left), reviews FLIR footage of his division's attack on Al Taqaddum air base. This strike was conducted several hours after Cdr Denneny's formation had hit the Ministry of Information's Salman Pak radio relay transmitter facility at Al Hurriyah at 2100 hrs on 21 March 2003. Cdr Whitson later received an Air Medal for his leadership of the Al Taqaddum mission, and an extract from the citation that accompanied this award read as follows;

'As Overall Commander of a five-ship package of Coalition strikers, Cdr Whitson masterfully led his attack into a complex surface-to-air missile engagement zone protecting Baghdad and successfully destroyed targets at the Al Taqaddum airfield. Cdr Whitson's strike was part of the Coalition effort to disrupt the enemy aviation arm in their most heavily defended sanctuaries in and around the Iraqi capital. Commander Whitson deftly managed his strike under fire, adjusting timing and delivery altitudes to react to enemy weapons systems and changing weather. Undaunted by the numerous barrages of anti-aircraft artillery fire and missile launches, the flight expertly delivered five Joint Direct Attack Munitions on target' (*PH2 Dan McLain*)

from our weapons were also evident, although the cloud partially obscured them. Then the normal admin issues came back into play – worrying about gas and weather at the tanker, making your recovery slot over the ship and, of course, the gratuitous night trap.'

Both Cdr Denneny and Lt Cdr Frankenberger subsequently received Distinguished Flying Crosses for the successful execution of this operation, as did their mission lead, Capt Fox, and one of the Hornet pilots in their section, Cdr Walt Stammer (CO of VFA-137).

Aside from the two VF-2 jets assigned to hit Salman Pak, a second section of 'Bounty Hunter' F-14Ds later attacked targets at the heavily defended Al Taqaddum air base to the west of Baghdad, dropping five 2000-lb JDAM that helped render the airfield inoperable – this mission was led by squadron CO, Cdr Andrew Whitson.

A single section of missile-armed F-14s had also launched from CV-64 with each strike package on the first night of 'Shock and Awe' in order to provide DCA for the CVW-2 jets as they headed into central Iraq. These aircraft boasted a traditional F-14 fighter load out, being equipped with pairs of AIM-54Cs, AIM-7Ms and AIM-9Ms. Strapped into the back of one of these jets was VF-2's most junior naval aviator, Lt(jg) Pat Baker;

'While my pilot and I were patrolling on our assigned CAP station, I spotted two Al Samoud 2 missiles being launched and heading south for Kuwait. We were trying to work out what they were, as they did not fly like SAMs. Their motors were much slower-burning, and once they had reached their apex they would flame out, disappearing from our view. We were on NVGs, so you could see the missiles' deep red rocket flash as they climbed away from the ground, and then they would go dark once the motor stopped. We could still see them on NVGs for a few seconds more, before they disappeared into the night.

'Keen to work out whether they were heading for our jet, it took us a few seconds to identify them as surface-to-surface missiles. According to our ROE, we had instructions to immediately report any such Scud, Al Samoud 2, FROG-7 or Ababil missile firings to the Patriot batteries via JTIDS, and they were weapons free to engage them.'

A third CVW-2 strike scheduled for the night of 21 March was eventually scrubbed short of the target due to poor weather over Baghdad.

One of the VF-2 F-14s launched as part of that mission was crewed entirely by CVW-2 staff officers, with Lt Cdr Dave Grogan flying the jet and deputy air wing commander Capt Craig Geron acting as his RIO. An ex-Intruder bombardier/navigator and Prowler Electronics Countermeasures Officer (who also flew several EA-6B sorties in OIF), Geron had transitioned onto the F-14 upon his assignment to CVW-2 in 2002. He recalled;

'Our strike was actually aborted due to bad weather when we had problems tanking. One of our

F/A-18s had a probe break off, and the jet had to divert to a shore base, and we also damaged the probe on our F-14. To make matters worse, our USAF F-16CJs showed up late. Although we eventually got into Iraq, we soon aborted due to the worsening weather.'

Lt Cdr Grogan also had some vivid memories of his first OIF mission;

'The thing that amazed me most about the first night of "Shock and Awe" was the sheer number of aircraft in the skies over Iraq. Everywhere you looked there were gaggles of jets heading north, and all of us were flying into bad weather. A couple of aircraft from CVW-2 suffered probe damage while refuelling in bad turbulence, and several more diverted to land bases in Kuwait when they could not plug into the tankers prior to running low on gas. DCAG Geron and I also had problems getting fuel.'

CVW-14 INTO ACTION

The only carrier-based assets to make it to Baghdad on 21 March had come from CV-64's CVW-2, as the entire follow-on CVW-14 strike package had been forced to abort due to a shortage of tankers. However, the second and third waves sent to hit targets in and around the Iraqi capital in the early hours of the 22nd included elements from CVN-72, and later that day still more F-14Ds, F/A-18Cs and F/A-18Es from *Lincoln* ventured into southern Iraq to attack targets listed on the ATO. CVW-14 CO Capt Kevin Albright was on one of those strikes;

'The mission called for four F/A-18Es and two F-14Ds to strike a missile production facility in the Karbala area, approximately 40 miles southwest of Baghdad. I was flying as "Dash 3" in the Super Hornet division. The ATO was well constructed by the CAOC, which had the huge task of coordinating and scheduling thousands of sorties every day. Tanker tracks, offload fuel amounts and timings were all spot on.

'The Super Hornets were loaded with a mix of 2000-lb JDAM that included a penetrator variety, as well as the standard Mk 84 bomb body. The F-14Ds were loaded up with two 2000-lb JDAM each. All strike fighter aircraft also carried a self-defence air-to-air load-out as well.

'Brief, man-up and launch went as planned. We were assigned a USAF KC-10, along with a US Marine Corps EA-6B which had launched from Prince Sultan Air Base in Saudi Arabia. In addition, we were also slated for a section of USAF F-16CJ SEAD-equipped fighters. Everyone was full-up, mission ready, on time and on station. No small feat, and a tribute to the CAOC's ATO planners and the maintainers in all the services who kept this huge armada airborne "24/7".

'Shortly after the strike package established communications with our AWACS controller, he advised us that an Iraqi bomber – a Tu-16 "Badger" – had been located at Al Taqaddum air base. This airfield was about 30 miles northwest of our assigned target. The controller

CVW-14's first night strikes in OIF were stymied by a lack of 'big wing' tanker support. Indeed, the latter were so hard to come by that the entire strike package was forced to turn around and return to CVN-72 with their bombs still on their racks. Leading the strike was VFA-25's XO, Cdr Don Braswell, who recalled;

'CVW-14 had been divided up into strike teams, and it just happened that my team was chosen to participate in the first strike on Baghdad. Prior to launching, we had told the CAOC that there was not going to be enough fuel on-station for everyone to press on into Iraq, and that was exactly what happened.'

Another naval aviator from *Lincoln* who felt the effects of the tanker shortage on 'A-Day' commented that 'The biggest limiting factor to the generation of sorties from our carrier in OIF was the availability of airborne gas in-theatre. The USAF, RAF and RAAF did their best I'm sure, but when we looked at trying to increase the number of sorties we were flying, we struggled to find the gas available to support the extra aircraft'. Fully fuelled, bombed up and awaiting their crew, these two F-14Ds (BuNos 164344 and 163904) from VF-31 are positioned on the fantail of CVN-72 on the eve of OIF. The RIO in the foreground is discussing the serviceability of his jet with a squadron maintainer, prior to conducting his pre-flight walkaround (*US Navy*)

passed coordinates for the bomber and we assigned them to the two Tomcats. The mission commander, the F-14D lead and the VF-31 CO (Cdr Paul Haas) quickly worked out a new timing plan en route which allowed the F-16CJs and EA-6B to provide coverage for both strike packages. The Tomcat crews also re-programmed the aim points in their JDAM thanks to the weapon's Target Of Opportunity (TOO) mode.

'As we flowed north toward the Baghdad area, I was surprised by how eerily quiet the radios were. I was also amazed at how tranquil the Iraq air defences seemed to be. We could see Baghdad as we approached from the southwest. When wearing NVGs, any weapons fired could easily be seen – there was no activity. That would soon change, however.

'As the Tomcats approached their targets, the F-16CJs prepared to launch several HARMs against Iraqi air defence radars. It was easy to see the missiles coming off the F-16CJs from our position some 20 miles southwest of their location – I was impressed by the sheer speed of the HARMs as they raced towards their targets. After their shots supporting the F-14Ds, the F-16CJs quickly repositioned southeast to protect the F/A-18Es. The Prowler aircrew had previously set up an orbit that allowed them to cover both targets nearly simultaneously.

'The Tomcats were on target just as we hit our initial point. The four Super Hornets had a great nose-on view of some of the most impressive secondary explosions I have ever witnessed. Clearly the Tomcats "shacked" the bomber, which appeared to be fully loaded with both fuel and ordnance. Those JDAM woke up the entire Al Taqaddum air defence force, because a huge barrage of AAA and ballistic SAMs began to streak skyward. Fortunately, the Tomcats were able to egress without taking any hits, although they did have at least one SAM come within several hundred yards of their flight as it split their section.

'I was impressed with the radio discipline from all the flights. Aircrew were calling SAMs and AAA in calm, clear voices, and keeping leads informed of their intentions. This allowed us to keep the flights together and continue to press home the attacks.

Configured as a TARPS jet in the opening stages of OIF, 'Tomcatter 101' was restricted to DCA sorties until fitted with an LTS pod as the ground war got into full swing. Seen flying a CAP for CVW-14 strikers soon after 'A-Day', the jet has just topped off its tanks from KC-135R 62-3505, assigned to the 22nd Air Refueling Wing's 344th Aerial Refueling Squadron. The latter unit was controlled by the 379th Air Expeditionary Wing at Al Udeid air base, in Qatar, during OIF. The USAF committed 149 KC-135s and 33 KC-10s to OIF, and between them, the two types flew 6193 sorties during the ground war. There was no shortage of customers for the 'big wing' tankers either, as these aircraft passed more fuel in OIF than in *Desert Storm*, despite there being one-third fewer tankers in-theatre in 2003 (*Lt Cdr Jim Muse*)

'The F/A-18Es hit their assigned target approximately three minutes behind the F-14Ds. Once we completed our off-count and verified that eight weapons had been released, the entire package began to egress southeast. The Super Hornet division observed multiple SAM launches on the way home, but none of us were illuminated by target tracking radars and none of the SAMs appeared to guide on us. We saw significant AAA in the southern Baghdad area, with many secondary explosions from a large Coalition strike that was underway.

'Our return to the post-mission tanking location was uneventful, and we recovered aboard *Abraham Lincoln* four hours after launching following a very satisfying mission.'

Like the VF-31 jets re-routed mid-mission in order to conduct the reactive strike on the Tu-16 at Al Taqaddum, VF-2 also had a section of aircraft pulled from a Baghdad-bound package on 22 March. Lt Cdrs Keith Kimberly (pilot) and David Hughes (RIO) were leading a mixed division of Tomcats, Hornets, F-16CJs and a Prowler towards southern Baghdad when they overheard on their radio that a US Army Blackhawk helicopter had come down in enemy territory not far from their present location. Kimberly quickly volunteered, via his AWACS controller, to act as the Rescue Mission Commander. He duly directed his section of F-14s over to the crash site, and once overhead the UH-60, made contact with the downed crewmen.

Having ascertained the physical condition and position of all crewmembers from the downed helicopter, Kimberly and Hughes swiftly brought together a Combat Search and Rescue package of more then ten aircraft. For the next two hours the naval aviators directed the coordination of assets necessary for the safe and expeditious recovery of the downed airmen, despite their aircraft being exposed to continuous hostile fire. Both Kimberly and Hughes duly received Air Medals for their exploits during the successful rescue of the entire Blackhawk crew.

Remaining in the thick of the action until war's end, Kimberly and Hughes would subsequently receive DFCs for a particularly challenging FAC(A) mission that they flew on 6 April near Baghdad International Airport. Only four DFCs were presented to Tomcat crewmen in the wake of OIF, and all of them were awarded to naval aviators from VF-2.

JDAM MONOPOLY

For the first three days of OIF, the 20 Tomcats of VF-2 and VF-31 sortied almost exclusively with two or three 2000-lb GBU-31s bolted onto the jets' modified Phoenix pallets. The F-14Ds' contribution to the brief 'Shock and Awe' phase of the conflict justified the effort that went into getting the aircraft JDAM-compatible in the final weeks of OSW. The aircrews also appreciated the simplicity of the system when it came to its employment in the particularly hostile skies over Iraq in the early phase of the campaign, as CVW-2's Lt Cdr Grogan confirmed;

'JDAM was such a simple system to use that you could almost have put a monkey in the front seat of a Tomcat and it would have flown a satisfactory mission profile to ensure the weapon's accurate delivery! Indeed, the actual targeting phase of the mission with this weapon was almost anti-climactic, which was just as well considering the level of AAA and SAM launches that were encountered in (*text continues on page 48*) 39

COLOUR PLATES

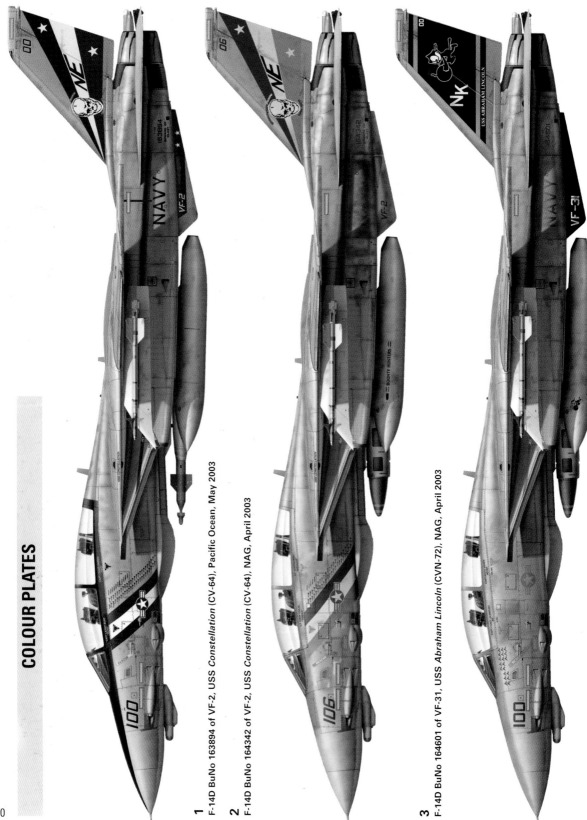

1
F-14D BuNo 163894 of VF-2, USS *Constellation* (CV-64), Pacific Ocean, May 2003

2
F-14D BuNo 164342 of VF-2, USS *Constellation* (CV-64), NAG, April 2003

3
F-14D BuNo 164601 of VF-31, USS *Abraham Lincoln* (CVN-72), NAG, April 2003

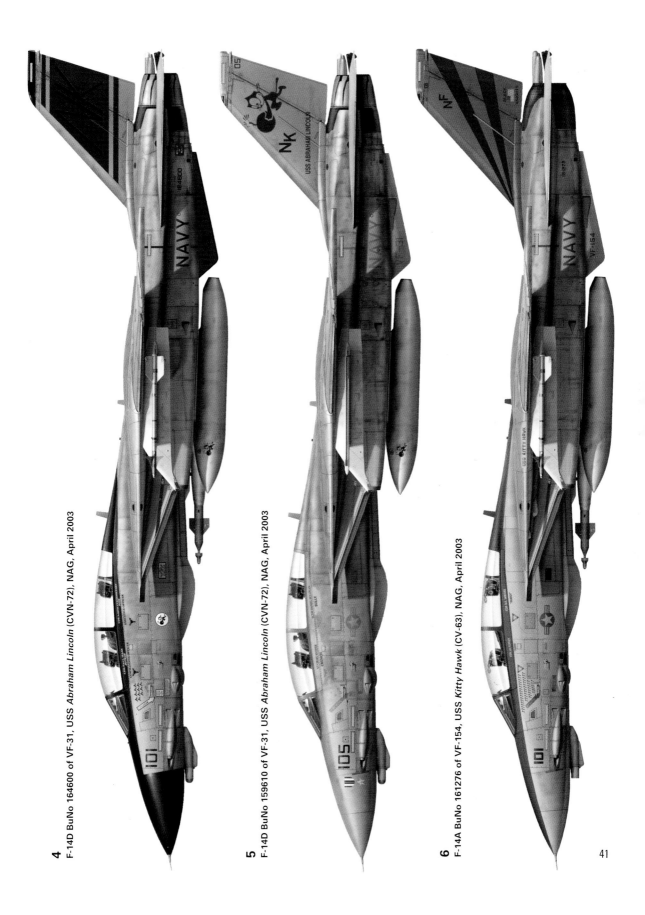

4

F-14D BuNo 164600 of VF-31, USS *Abraham Lincoln* (CVN-72), NAG, April 2003

5

F-14D BuNo 159610 of VF-31, USS *Abraham Lincoln* (CVN-72), NAG, April 2003

6

F-14A BuNo 161276 of VF-154, USS *Kitty Hawk* (CV-63), NAG, April 2003

41

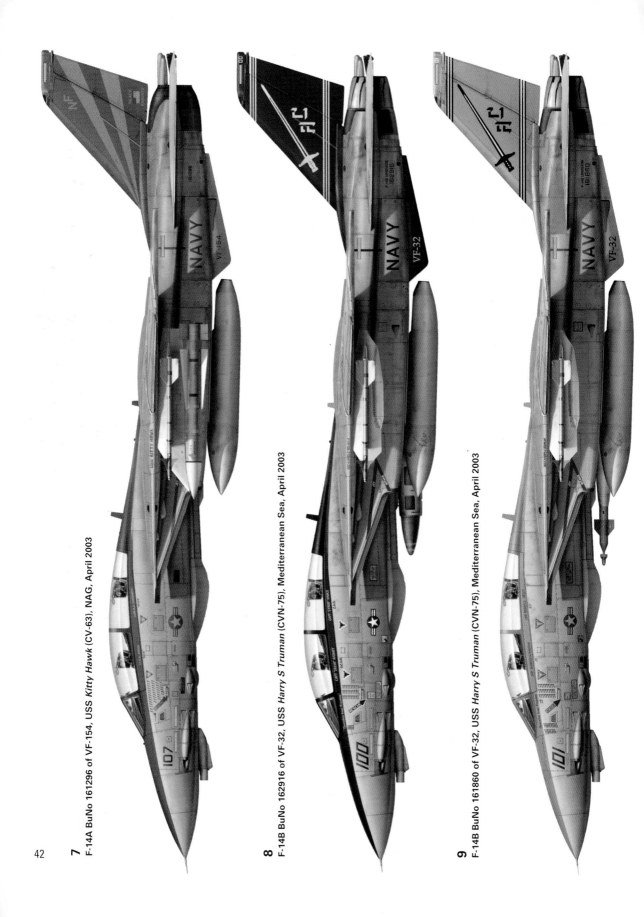

7
F-14A BuNo 161296 of VF-154, USS *Kitty Hawk* (CV-63), NAG, April 2003

8
F-14B BuNo 162916 of VF-32, USS *Harry S Truman* (CVN-75), Mediterranean Sea, April 2003

9
F-14B BuNo 161860 of VF-32, USS *Harry S Truman* (CVN-75), Mediterranean Sea, April 2003

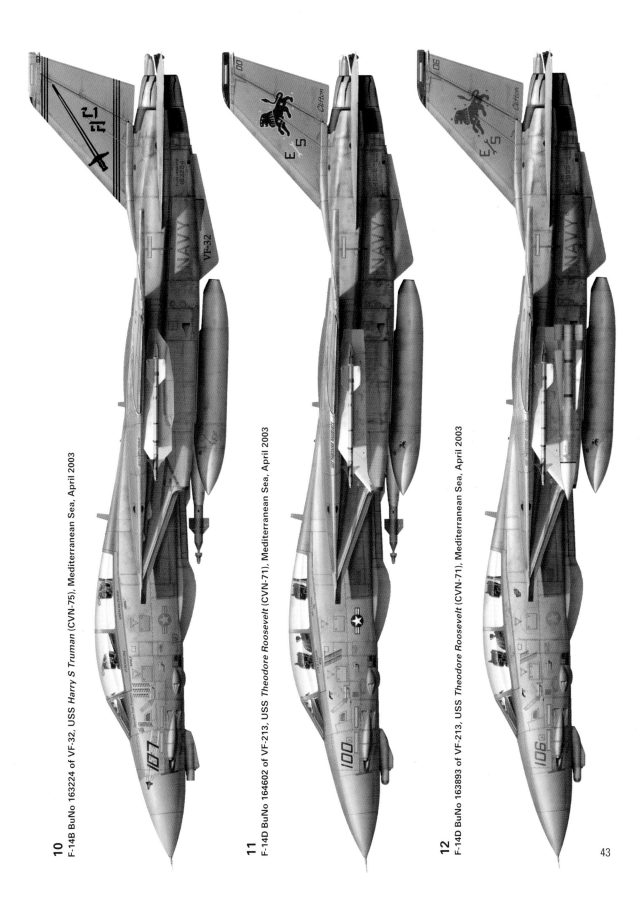

10
F-14B BuNo 163224 of VF-32, USS *Harry S Truman* (CVN-75), Mediterranean Sea, April 2003

11
F-14D BuNo 164602 of VF-213, USS *Theodore Roosevelt* (CVN-71), Mediterranean Sea, April 2003

12
F-14D BuNo 163893 of VF-213, USS *Theodore Roosevelt* (CVN-71), Mediterranean Sea, April 2003

43

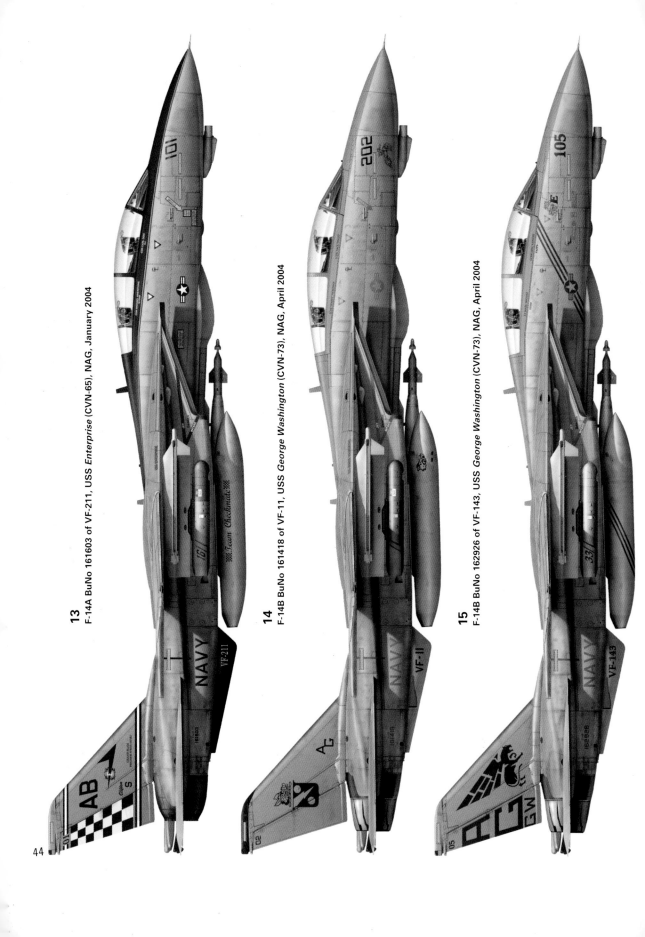

13
F-14A BuNo 161603 of VF-211, USS *Enterprise* (CVN-65), NAG, January 2004

14
F-14B BuNo 161418 of VF-11, USS *George Washington* (CVN-73), NAG, April 2004

15
F-14B BuNo 162926 of VF-143, USS *George Washington* (CVN-73), NAG, April 2004

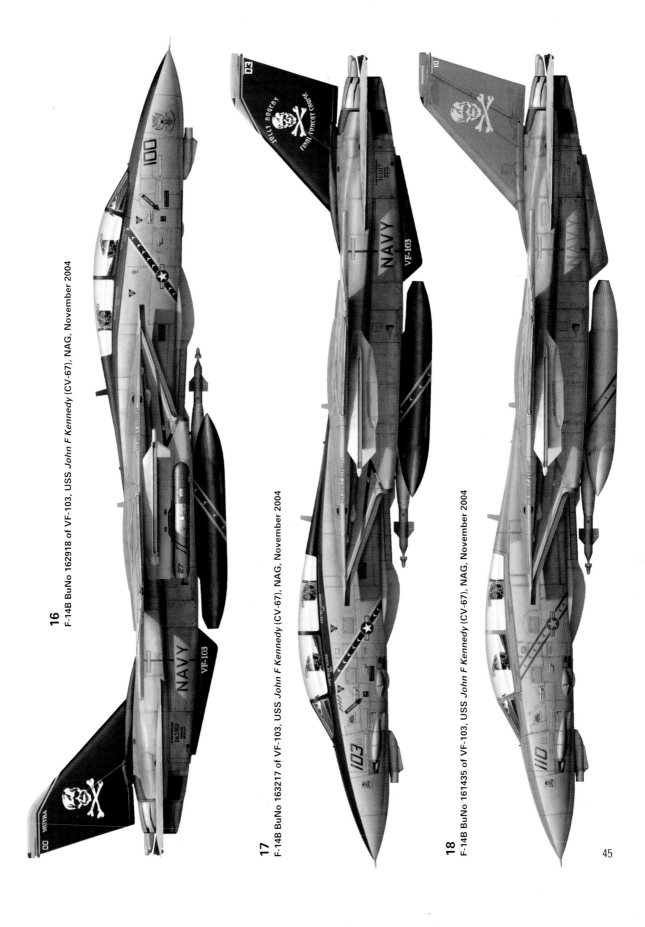

16
F-14B BuNo 162918 of VF-103, USS *John F Kennedy* (CV-67), NAG, November 2004

17
F-14B BuNo 163217 of VF-103, USS *John F Kennedy* (CV-67), NAG, November 2004

18
F-14B BuNo 161435 of VF-103, USS *John F Kennedy* (CV-67), NAG, November 2004

1

NK

USS ABRAHAM LINCOLN

5

105

4

USS ABRAHAM LINCOLN

8

4

CDR PAUL HAA
BUTKUS

COMMANDING

RESCUE

9

3

10

107

Operation Iraqi Freedom

RESCUE

11

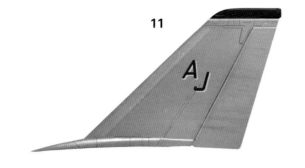

14

11

CAPT. S. J. Laukaitis
DCAG

16

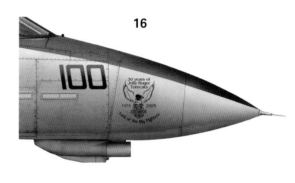

16

12

LT Tony Towse
Elroy

17

"Shock and Awe". The most important aspect of a JDAM mission for the crew was making sure that we had the target coordinates correctly copied down – these were given to us either in the pre-launch brief or once we were over Iraq. Both the RIO and I would double-check the coordinates before they were dialled into the bomb via the mission computer. From my OSW/OIF experience, I would suggest that the only weak point in the whole JDAM system is the data entry phase.

'The actual drop zone for the JDAM from its maximum range to minimum range was usually quite large, so we would take it to the heart of the target area whenever possible before hitting the release switch. In the Tomcat community, we were so used to having to visually identify the target with the LTS and the FLIR before hitting the "pickle button" to release an LGB that it initially felt rather odd to be expending JDAM through solid cloud against targets that we never saw.

'Aside from its incredible accuracy against fixed targets, the JDAM also proved to be ultra reliable in combat. We would check the weapons' interaction with the jet on deck as soon as we had strapped in, and any degradation in the bombs' ability to read the GPS coordinates correctly would become immediately obvious during our pre-flight test. We always had at least one spare jet bombed up ready to go just in case we experienced a serviceability issue with a primary aircraft pre-launch. I was forced to swap jets just once in OIF when we got a "bad" bomb from the ship's magazine. It refused to interact with the F-14, so we simply swapped aircraft and still made the launch cycle.'

Lt Cdr Jim Muse of CVW-14, who also got to employ GPS weapons towards the end of 'Shock and Awe', told the Author that aircrew would typically conduct much of their mission weaponeering with JDAM prior to walking to the jet;

'With JDAM, the real effort came in the pre-flight planning rather than over the target, as was the case with the LGB. There were several different JDAM attack profiles I could choose from once airborne, depending on the target being serviced. If I had a vertical target, I wanted the weapon to come in at a low angle, and if I had a horizontal target, then I wanted it to hit at a steep angle. We had a pattern of deliveries for different altitudes,

Bombs gone, a VF-2 striker pairs up with an AIM-54C-toting DCA jet in the marshall overhead CV-64 at the end of an early 'Shock and Awe' mission. Few naval aviators assigned to VF-2 in OIF got to see the sun during flight operations, as CVW-2 was operating from CTF-50's designated night carrier. According to Lt Cdr Mike Peterson, '"Late" missions were a double-edged sword for the aircrew of VF-2. As the NAG night carrier during OIF, the entire ship turned their schedule upside-down in an attempt to adjust the aircrew's circadian rhythm to night operations. The crew ate breakfast at about 1830 hrs, lunch at midnight, dinner in the morning and slept during most daylight hours. Being on the later portion of the ATO schedule would have the aircraft landing at, or after, sunrise. While the day trap was a welcomed change from the night version, after seeing the sun it took days to trick your body into living like a vampire again' (*VF-2*)

and we could match these up to suit the target being attacked. VF-31 crews usually knew what they were going after beforehand, and configured the JDAM accordingly prior to launching, but the weapon's TOO mode was flexible enough to allow for airborne coordinate changes should the mission requirements alter mid-sortie.

'I got to put this flexibility to the test when I dropped my first JDAM of OIF. Although VF-31 had mostly flown fixed strikes for the first few days of the war, by the time I went into action on 23 March, we had begun moving into the CAS phase of the campaign. We had also been given a "dump target" list by then, which contained the coordinates for things like bunkers, buildings and known SAM sites. We could work down this seemingly endless list if we could not find anyone on the ground who needed our bombs to support their advance to Baghdad.

'Upon our arrival over southern Iraq, we checked in with AWACS, who directed us to a location at which tanks had been reported. We scoured the area where they told us they would be, but couldn't find any tanks, so we told our controller that we had DMPIs (Designated Mean Point of Impact) from the dump list and requested permission to attack those instead. This was approved in short order and we headed north for the targets.

'This was at the beginning of the bad sandstorms that clobbered the area, and visibility was absolutely horrid. We were lucky to find our mission tanker – a VFA-115 Super Hornet from our own boat – on the way in. Flying towards the target, we knew that there were other jets out there, but we sure couldn't see them. We only had datalink with our wingman – no visual reference – and we just stuck to our designated altitude and prayed! It was one of the scariest missions I've ever flown. We dropped our JDAM from 32,000 ft in complete brown-out conditions, felt the bomb drop away, and turned for home. I assume that we hit the target, but we never did find that out for sure.

'On our way home we were contacted by some Marines who were looking for a jet to fly a low-level road reconnaissance for them. They asked us to look for tanks that they thought were on the north side of a town that they were approaching. We dropped down low and fast, pumping lots of chaff as we went because we could never tell where MANPADS (Man-Portable Air Defence System) would show up. We made a high-speed, low-level pass along a river and over a small pontoon bridge, on which I spotted numerous people. Startled by our low pass, they fled in all directions away from the bridge, which they assumed we were going to bomb.

'It was very bumpy down low, the visibility was not brilliant, and I have to admit it was a little scary to be flying well within the enemy's AAA and SAM engagement zone – I had never flown so low over Iraq before. If the weather had been better, we could have just scoured the area through our LTS from a nice safe 20,000 ft. We couldn't find any tanks here either, so we went home and the Marines eventually pushed through.'

The 'Shock and Awe' phase of OIF had effectively run its course by the time a series of sandstorms of near-biblical proportion rolled into southern Iraq and the NAG on 25 March. From then on, most Tomcat crews would be supporting the troops on the ground as the latter raced towards Baghdad.

SHAPING THE BATTLEFIELD

As briefly detailed in the previous chapter, the prosecution of the Coalition's OPLAN 1003V called for the ground war to start after several days of sustained bombing against key fixed targets in Iraq. However, this plan ended up being compressed to such a degree that 'G-Day', as the ground invasion was designated, actually preceded 'A-Day'. With mechanised troops from the US Army's V Corps and the US Marine Corps' 1st MEF racing into southern Iraq from Kuwait, hell-bent on reaching Baghdad as quickly as possible, the CAOC was hastily forced to switch its focus from destroying fixed targets to conducting Kill box Interdiction Close Air Support (KI/CAS) and Battlefield Air Interdiction (BAI) sorties.

Much thought had gone into how best to control TACAIR assets in OIF once the ground war got into full swing, with Gen Tommy Franks challenging his war planners to integrate as many air assets as they could into an overall network of 'joint fires' that directly supported ground force commanders heading north. CENTCOM staffers duly employed the Fire Support Coordination Line (FSCL) concept, which delineated a moving line up to which the 'joint fire' assets – jets, attack helicopters and artillery – were under the control of ground force commanders in the field, and beyond which they fell under the jurisdiction of the Joint Force Air Component Commander (JFACC).

Anyone could engage targets that were positively identified as enemy military units beyond the FSCL without real-time coordination with ground units, while targets short of the FSCL had to be coordinated with the ground commander in whose AOR the target was situated. The kill box system, detailed elsewhere in this chapter, was used to make the process of updating the FSCL easier, as it allowed the latter to change rapidly without the reissuing of coordinates that defined the line.

This was a radical plan, as traditionally all fixed wing strikers had been controlled exclusively by the JFACC in a time of conflict. Gen Franks placed even more faith in his senior officers on the ground by opting for a 'deep FCSL' once the invasion commenced, this seeing Army or Marine divisional commanders controlling all 'joint fires' out to a range of 100 miles. The value of this extended FCSL was quickly realised when the rapid advances in the south saw friendly forces crossing the 'joint fire' line. Had the TACAIR assets committed to CAS been controlled by the JFACC only, then the potential for friendly fire incidents could have been huge due to AWACS controllers not being fully aware of how far ground forces had advanced north.

In an effort to allow the JFACC to also play its part in the 'deep FCSL' strategy, CENTCOM devised the kill box system. This saw a ground commander split up his area of responsibility into 18.5-mile x 18.5-mile boxes, which he would then declare 'closed' when his troops entered them. Such a system shifted the 'joint fires' responsibility from the JFACC to the ground commander, thus reducing the chance of 'blue-on-blue' fratricide. When a kill box was declared 'open', the JFACC would assume that it was clear of friendly forces, thus allowing Coalition TACAIR to prosecute enemy targets.

KI/CAS became a key mission as V Corps and the 1st MEF pushed further north, with both forces deliberately manoeuvring around strong points in towns such as An Nasiriyah, Al Kut and An Najaf in an effort to get to Baghdad as quickly as possible in true *Blitzkrieg* style. Air power was the chosen means of keeping these pockets of enemy fighters holed up in the southern and central towns while US forces rapidly headed north.

The kill boxes opened up a fixed area that was usually short of the FSCL where targets could be attacked by TACAIR assets without direct coordination with ground units. As the 1st MEF and V Corps moved rapidly northward, the FSCLs marched north with them. Kill boxes were opened on their flanks, where no friendly forces remained, to allow air power to eliminate threats in these vulnerable areas.

Beyond the FCSL, the JFACC continued to 'shape the battlefield' in advance of the mechanised troops through the CAOC-controlled BAI sorties. Such missions included pre-planned attacks on mechanised troop concentrations held in reserve, reveted armour around Baghdad and the selective destruction of bridges so as to stop Republican Guard forces south of the Iraqi capital retreating into the city itself.

As many as 2000 sorties a day were flown as part of CAS/BAI effort at the height of OIF, with the bulk of these being sent against the forces of the Republican Guard squeezed into the Karbala-Baghdad-Al Kut triangle. Thanks to the Coalition's highly effective combined arms strategy that had seen ground forces working closer with TACAIR than ever before, the 2 Medina, 1 Hammurabi and 5 Baghdad Divisions could not disperse their armoured and mechanised elements for fear of engagement by marauding M1A1/2 Abrams tanks and attack helicopters. Concentrating in force was the only defence left open to the Republican Guard, yet this in turn played into the hands of orbiting strike aircraft flying over the battlefield.

With ground forces hastily pushing north while 'Shock and Awe' was still underway, some senior naval aviators felt that the switch from fixed target strikes to CAS was not handled as well as it could have been. CVW-2's DCAG, Capt Craig Geron was one such critic;

'The speed at which the Army and Marines headed for Baghdad caught the CAOC out, as it struggled to keep up with the ground war in terms of switching TACAIR assets over from fixed strikes to CAS. The E-2s really came into their own during this early stage of the land war, as they took on the task of keeping TACAIR crews in-theatre informed of the evolving ATO, which was literally being shaped by the minute according to ongoing requirements on the ground.

'For E-2 controllers, running a CAS mission in the first week of the war could be equated to overseeing the operation of a marketplace, where you have sellers and buyers. TACAIR assets were the sellers, having product in the form of ordnance on aeroplanes. It took time to sort through the

frequencies to work out who needed this highly perishable commodity at what time. The E-2 controller acted as the go-between, ensuring the troops on the ground got what that wanted both quickly and efficiently.'

Conspiring against this 'on time delivery' of ordnance was the administrative control matrix governing all TACAIR crews in OIF. VF-2's Lt Cdr Mike Peterson recalled;

'As you approached Iraqi airspace, you would have to check-in with multiple agencies who, on occasion, did not effectively pass information to the next agency. First check-in was done in the NAG with the over water controller, followed by a call to the Kuwait Contact Reporting Centre, then the east lane AWACS, then the tanking AWACS, then the tanker itself, then the middle lane AWACS, then either the ASOC (Air Support Operations Center for V Corps) or the DASC (Direct Air Support Center for the 1st MEF), then the actual ground unit to be supported if you were not assigned a kill box. Upon speaking with each of these controllers for the first time, we had to start the check-in procedure all over again. This made it a long, slow and very frustrating process getting to the end user.

'Additionally, there was a roughly north-south line that divided V Corps (Army) battlespace from that controlled by the 1st MEF

Below
VF-2's CAG jet was in the thick of the action during OSW/OIF dropping some 49 LGBs and ten JDAM during the conflict. Delivered to the Navy on 30 September 1990, BuNo 163894 initially served with VF-124 at Miramar. It was then assigned to VF-101 Det West when VF-124 disbanded in September 1994. The aircraft entered fleet service with VF-2 in October 1997, and completed the unit's 1999 *WestPac* as 'Bullet 106'. Pulled from service in 2000 for scheduled deep maintenance, BuNo 163894 returned to VF-2 in late 2001 when it replaced BuNo 163901 as 'Bullet 100' following the 'Bounty Hunter's' *WestPac* of that year. Having completed VF-2's OSW/OIF cruise, the aircraft was one of a handful of 'Bounty Hunter' jets assigned to VF-101 following the unit's transition to the F/A-18F (*VF-2*)

Opposite left
The pilot of 'Bullet 104' (BuNo 163900) deploys his tailhook so that his wingman can check its operability prior to descending into a thick undercast for recovery aboard CV-64. The jet is devoid of bombs, having released its ordnance during a SCAR mission over southern Iraq in late March 2003. Cdr Doug Denneny and Lt Cdr Kurt Frankenberger had used the jet to attack a radio site near H3 air base, west of Al Rutbah, in the early hours of 21 March, this being the very last VF-2 strike of OSW. It went on to drop 16 LGBs and 22 JDAM in OIF. Delivered new to VF-124 at Miramar on 24 March 1991, BuNo 163900 was transferred to VF-11 in 1993. It remained with the 'Red Rippers' as part of CVW-14 until the unit replaced it F-14Ds with B-model Tomcats and transferred to CVW-7 in 1997. The aircraft was passed on to VF-31, which retained its F-14Ds as CVW-14's sole Tomcat unit. Completing just one *WestPac* with the 'Tomcatters', BuNo 163900 joined VF-2 in 1999 and undertook a further three deployments as 'Bullet 104'. Following VF-2's switch to the F/A-18F in mid 2003, the jet was transferred to VF-101, with whom it is still serving today (*VF-2*)

Although CVW-14 was the dedicated day air wing in the NAG, its flying time lasted from noon through to midnight, so some of its missions were flown after dark. This LGB-equipped F-14D from VF-31 is heading south in search of a tanker mid-way through a CAS mission (*Lt Cdr Jim Muse*)

(Marine). Amazingly, by doctrine, these two services have different organisations and agencies to effect the support of ground troops. The Army ASOC (call-sign "Warhawk") was often a dead end if you were tasked to support the ground units as a CAS player or FAC(A). The "Warhawk" controllers often seemed surprised that you had shown up to support them, even though you were listed on the ATO sent out to everyone in-theatre by the CAOC! They did not make effective use of FAC(A) aircrew, and had CAS assets in support of a ground unit that could have used an airborne FAC to assist in providing situational awareness and the organisation of asset flow into their area.

'The DASC, conversely, was excellent at assigning the correct CAS and FAC(A) assets with the ground units that needed support based on ordnance, capabilities and on-station time. If there were no units that required help during your assigned on-station time, they would get you to an open kill box that was known to be clear of all blue forces and allow you to operate as a SCAR or armed reconnaissance asset, hitting targets that were positively identified as enemy forces within the established RoE.

'Bottom line – you had to actively work the system so as to get to where you were needed, and do it expeditiously so that you had a significant amount of time on-station in the vicinity of the troops on the ground. Operating as part of a FAC(A)-qualified crew, my pilot and I often found ourselves pushing a plan to the AWACS controllers that ensured that the right TACAIR assets showed up at the correct places. In order to achieve this, we often took the requests from the ground controllers and helped solve the asset allocation process ourselves by letting the AWACS know who was on-station with the required ordnance, and what frequency they were working. The E-2 was great at keeping track of who was where, and we often used J-Voice as our backdoor link to the Hawkeye to get our problems solved.

'J-Voice was just one of several excellent comms systems – including the all-seeing Link-16 JTIDS – fitted into the F-14D that made the jet the ultimate FAC(A) platform. Our aircraft had the capability to gain up to two voice channels, depending on how the particular network was structured. This gave the F-14D two UHF/VHF radios capable of secure comms, and two additional radios for J-Voice. We would use one as an extra inter-flight comms channel because it was crystal clear, and you

could turn it up louder than the other radios for things that need immediate safety of flight or section keeping attention.

'We used the other radio to monitor the command net so that we had a backdoor through which to get a hold of the AWACS or E-2 controller when there wasn't free time on the regular frequency, you had lost them during a frequency change or if one of us dropped out of sync. More than once, we dialled up the check-in frequency and heard more than ten sections of aircraft repeatedly attempting to contact the AWACS on an assigned frequency, and we in turn had to call the AWACS on J-Voice and let them know that they had dropped sync on the radio – to which they usually replied, "I thought that it was kind of quiet lately"! Ten seconds later they would come up on the original net, back in sync with the rest of the world.

'In many cases the AWACS controllers seemed overwhelmed with responding to the situation on the ground and effectively getting the correct assets to the correct location at the correct time. In their defence, they were not used to managing air assets in support of a ground war. They were very adept at managing CAPs, and the overall air picture, but were trying to fill the ABCCC (Air Borne Command and Control Centre) role that was usually handled by other mission crews.

'J-Voice was also great for letting you know what was going to happen before it was put out over normal channels. By listening to the command net, we would know when strikes were going to get moved back in time, and who was going to put in a request for support. If you had a Hornet wingman, he often thought that you were psychic – none of the F/A-18Cs in-theatre had J-Voice . We routinely received calls like, "Hey, how did you guys know to head over toward that kill box before it opened?"'

VF-31 also experienced FAC problems during the early stages of the ground war, as CVW-14 staff RIO Lt Cdr Jim Muse recalled;

'We struggled a little early on in OIF when supporting the Army almost certainly because of the inexperience of its FACs. Our guys would show up over the battlefield with limited on-station time, and the FACs on the ground couldn't get them targets before they had to either find a tanker or head home. It seemed that the Army FACs were used to working with attack helicopters, which operate at slower speeds than tactical jets. This resulted in many guys coming back to the ship with their bombs still on the racks because of coordination problems with the troops on the ground in southern Iraq.

'We would then go down to the squadron ready rooms to be greeted by live CNN news reports stating that "the troops on the ground need more ordnance NOW!" Yet, when we had checked in with the Army FACs in-country less than two hours earlier, they had told us that they didn't need our bombs! Some guys resorted to independently dialling frequencies on the jet's radios and finding FACs that needed bombs, circumventing the designated process of who got what ordnance. This caused some hate and discontent in figuring out the process, but a number of VF-31 crews managed to find troops who needed bombs that way in the early stages of the war.'

CVW-2's DCAG Capt Craig Geron had some sympathy for the Army FACs he encountered during OIF, despite being routinely frustrated in his efforts to get bombs on targets;

'The standard Army FACs had no fancy equipment to help them do their job in often trying weather conditions in Iraq. The SOF guys that I occasionally worked with, on the other hand, all had the latest Viper laser systems that gave you solid coordinates. These fellows had also seen much action working with Navy TACAIR in Afghanistan in 2001-02, and had been trained in the tactics used by fast jet crews. Lacking this equipment or experience, the Army FACs often had to talk you onto targets, as they were unable to give you accurate coordinates. It was obvious to me that they were struggling. I found the whole situation immensely frustrating, as you could hear that your FAC was getting shot at while he was trying to get your eyes onto the target, which you in turn could not see!

'To make matters worse, often right next to where he wanted you to drop your bomb was a road full of cars, or civilian-occupied housing. In the back of your mind, you would be asking yourself "Is this really the right target, and is this really what the FAC wants me to do?"'

FAC(A) REVOLUTION

Navy and Marine Corps units have always been great proponents of working with forward air controllers operating from fast jet types. Known as Forward Air Controller (Airborne), the lineage of the FAC(A) goes back to Vietnam, when Marine 'spotters' performed the Tactical Air Controlling (Airborne) mission in aircraft such as the TF-9J Cougar and TA-4F Skyhawk. Today, the Marines still conduct the FAC(A) mission with their two-seat F/A-18Ds, which proved indispensable in the ground campaign of OIF.

The Navy got into the FAC(A) role a little later than the Marines, selecting the F-14 Tomcat for the mission following the aircraft's metamorphosis into a precision bomber in the mid 1990s. The only two-seat TACAIR jet then operating from a carrier deck that possessed the range, speed, targeting equipment, avionics and radios capable of performing this highly demanding role, the F-14 made its FAC(A) combat debut over Kosovo in Operation *Allied Force* in March 1999. The leading role played by US naval aviation in Operation *Enduring Freedom* two years later saw the Tomcat FAC(A) concept prove its worth over and over again. Much was therefore expected of the F-14 units committed to OIF in the NAG in March 2003, and they fulfilled all expectations.

CVW-2's DCAG select Capt Larry Burt, who flew as a CTF-50 staffer from CVN-72, before finishing the war flying from the deck of CV-64, was full of praise for the Tomcat FAC(A)s that he worked with over Iraq;

'When us Hornet guys were desperately trying to acquire and prosecute targets, the Tomcat FAC(A)s really came into their own. You had lots of jets ready to drop their bombs, but there was a shortage of real targets amongst all the potential contacts that needed to be attacked. It was therefore up to the FAC(A)s to work out what were the bona fide targets by talking over the radio with the guys on the ground, liaising with airborne controllers and scouring the battlefield with their own systems. It was while performing the SCAR and FAC(A) missions that the two-man crew in the Tomcat excelled. A big part of the FAC(A) mission is awareness, which comes with experience, and all of the FAC(A)-qualified crews had experience in abundance.'

Below
This VF-2 jet has been armed with two GBU-16s (left) and a solitary GBU-12 in preparation for its next mission from CV-64 in early April 2003. The aircraft is restricted to a top speed of around 470 mph when configured in this way, as increased airflow buffeting from the forward-mounted LGBs will damage the laser seeker head on the rear weapon, potentially rendering it unguidable when dropped. The bomb release sequencing in the F-14 sees the rear weapons 'pickled' first. If the forward bombs were released first, there could be an impact with the rear weapons as the forward weapon rapidly decelerates and deploys its stabilisation fins. During OIF, FAC(A)-manned jets usually launched with four LGBs aboard, while normal crews would typically sortie in F-14s bombed up with two or three GBU-12s. The load-out on this jet is unusual, as VF-2 only dropped four GBU-16s during OIF

VF-2 had five complete FAC(A) crews within its ranks, these pilots and RIOs having undertaken specialised training courses run by the Naval Strike Air Warfare Center (NSAWC) and the Strike Fighter Weapons School Atlantic (SFWSL) at places such as NASs Fallon and El Centro. Prior to receiving FAC(A) training, each Navy aircrew is qualified as a ground JTAC (Joint Tactical Air Controller, which is a revised term brought in post-OIF) following the completion of a three-week Tactical Air Control Party course run by the Marine Corps at EWTGLANT/PAC (Expeditionary Warfare Training Group Atlantic/ Pacific). These courses have to be passed to achieve the coveted FAC(A) qualification, with the designation of FAC(A) itself being the ultimate achievement – such a qualification is viewed as a doctorate in CAS by the Navy.

The VF-2 became the primary FAC(A) resource in the NAG thanks to the influx of several augment aircrew (a pilot and two RIOs) for OIF. Veteran fleet naval aviators who had been serving as instructors with the SFWSL prior to being sent out at short notice to the unit, they had been hand-picked to help VF-2 undertake SOF-related FAC(A) missions. Although the SFWSL augmentees sometimes flew together, they were usually paired up with other squadron FAC(A) pilots and RIOs in order to spread their expertise across a section of aircraft. The instructors also flew standard combat missions, helped out with the unpopular alerts and stood watches aboard CV-64. They were truly integrated into CVW-2, although their primary focus was the FAC(A) mission.

Thanks to the F-14D boasting Link-16 JTIDS and the AN/ALQ-165 Airborne Self-Protection Jammer, VF-2 was assigned to support what were arguably the most dynamic TACAIR missions of OIF – the secretive Time Critical Target (TCT) sorties flown for Task Force 20. These very long, dangerous and incredibly important FAC(A) missions required exceptional situational awareness in a joint environment – something that the

Opposite left
'Tomcatter 110' (BuNo 159618) is carrying two GBU-12s on its forward tunnel weapons rails, and possibly two more in the aft troughs too – the belly tanks and engine bays effectively mask the presence of the latter bombs except when directly beneath the Tomcat. The GBU-12 was the F-14's preferred weapon when supporting the ground war, VF-31 expending no fewer than 161 of the 464 dropped by CVW-14's four TACAIR units, while VF-2 delivered 217 of the 423 GBU-12s dropped by CVW-2's quartet of TACAIR units. BuNo 159618 expended 35 JDAM/LGBs (VF-31's mission marks did not differentiate between the two), and it was also involved in at least one strafing attack which saw it fire 193 20 mm cannon rounds. Originally built as an F-14A and delivered to VF-124 on 24 October 1975, BuNo 159618 was the 17th of 18 A-models rebuilt as F-14Ds in 1990-91. Following a second spell with VF-124 and then VF-101, the jet was assigned to VF-31 in 1995. It remained with the unit until 2 June 2003, when the aircraft was stricken and given over to SARDIP at NAS Oceana (*Lt Cdr Jim Muse*)

The naval aviators of VF-2 pose for a group shot in early May 2003 (PH2 Dan McLain)

older F-14As in the NAG were physically unable to provide. The combination of the F-14D's capabilities and VF-2's SFWSL-boosted FAC(A) crews saw the unit become the 'go-to' FAC(A) asset in OIF. Suitably qualified crews were routinely 'fragged' on the ATO to fly in and act as the 'quarterbacks' for some of the most dangerous and tactically demanding sorties of the conflict.

The TCT/TF-20 missions that VF-2 participated in involved SOF squads taking out targets of opportunity (key individuals in the Iraqi leadership, mobile radar/SAM sites and surface-to-surface missiles). Such elusive targets could present themselves only fleetingly anywhere across the country, and the SOF teams needed the ability to infiltrate, hit the target with overwhelming force, and depart under the cover of blinding firepower and complete darkness.

As the target lists were put together pre-war, it was realised that many of the prime missions would originate in and around the Baghdad SuperMEZ. SOF MC-130s and helicopter aircrew tasked with inserting and supporting the TF-20 squads requested dedicated, responsive fires over and above their organic capabilities to support these dangerous missions. The only ordnance that could reach deep into Iraqi airspace, and be flexible enough to meet their needs, would have to be delivered from Coalition TACAIR assets performing the CAS mission.

In the autumn of 2002, SOF air planners joined forces with conventional Marine Corps, Air Force and Navy aircrews who were subject matter experts (SMEs) on Joint CAS (JCAS) and FAC(A) procedures to provide a detailed concept of operations (CONOPs) on how conventional FAC and CAS jets would escort SOF aircraft to and from their targets in a robust high-threat environment. The CONOPs also detailed measures to provide fire support and assistance to SOF ground FACs during actions on their objectives.

The CONOPs was then validated by those same aircrew, who put their ideas to the test against Air Force and Navy weapons ranges simulating enemy threat systems. Face-to-face briefings and, more importantly, debriefings were stressed due to the fact that most SOF-to-conventional air forces interaction ended up being 'pick-up' games played on the battlefield, with both players 'arriving at the court' with the playbook (JCAS) already memorised.

After the rehearsals were over, the FAC(A) and CAS aircrew that practised the missions were alerted that they would be assigned to units already in-theatre under JTF-SWA control in order to teach what they had learned to the deployed crews. When theatre commanders learned of how well the rehearsals were executed, the aircrew were directed to lead the missions as 'tactical quarterbacks', integrating other Coalition FAC(A) and CAS aircraft into the SOF missions.

Night-operations based aircraft carriers (including *Constellation*) were preferred for the TF-20 sorties. This duly meant that VF-2 FAC(A)s and their augment aircrew led numerous missions ranging from the seizures of H2 and H3 airfields in western Iraq on the eve of OIF, to providing air support for a SOF takedown of an Iraqi Presidential palace on the shores of Lake Tharthar, northwest of Baghdad, towards the end of the conflict.

URBAN WARFARE

The VF-2 FAC(A)s really came into their own once Coalition troops started their assault on Baghdad itself. One of the RIOs heavily involved in this crucial stage of the campaign was Lt Cdr Mike Peterson, a veteran of OEF with CVW-11's VF-213;

'In the pre-dawn hours of 10 April, Lt Cdr Jeff Ohman and I launched off of *Constellation*, which we affectionately called "Satan's Flagship" – being one of the last conventional carriers, it always had a head of "Brimstone" streaming out of the top stacks.

'Due to our wingman suffering mechanical problems, and higher priority missions being filled by the spare Tomcat, we proceeded on our mission as a FAC(A) as a single aircraft. Working as a FAC(A), you usually had mutual support from the other CAS aircraft operating in any particular area, and having two sets of eyes in the cockpit helped our lookout for surface fires.

'After refuelling, we were assigned to a kill box by the DASC in support of a 1st MEF convoy that was working just east of the Tigris River in downtown Baghdad. As we headed on station, I pulled out a 1:50,000 chart and noted the coordinates where we were tasked to be working. It was a location in a dense urban area, just east of a bridge crossing the Tigris. I marked the location on the chart and used the Tomcat's "moving map feature" to show it to the pilot – in other words, I handed the map with my writing on it up the right side of the cockpit to my pilot!

'When we arrived on-station, we were contacted by a section of A-10 Warthogs that had just checked in as CAS assets. The convoy had stopped about a block east of the bridge and had surrounded what appeared to be a mosque. There were the typical spires and a significant wall surrounding the complex, which was located on the southwest side of an intersection. Apparently, the Marines were planning on looking for high-level Iraqi regime members that may have been hiding in the buildings.

'Immediately prior to our arrival overhead, the column had been fired on by heavy weapons and rocket-propelled grenades from the group of buildings located to the east side of the complex, across the street at their rear flank. They had sustained some casualties, and were trying to talk the A-10 onto the location of the heaviest fire as the troops pulled back toward the bridge.

'We quickly checked in as a FAC(A) and put the LTS to work scouring the mosque complex. We saw the buildings where the enemy fire was coming from after listening to the talk-on by the ground FAC. We were unable to drop our LGBs onto these buildings, however, as the Marines were still nearby, conducting their withdrawal from the area. The A-10 pilot was having a difficult time picking out the correct area to strafe, so we coordinated with the ground FAC and jumped in with a quick talk-on from the aerial perspective, dictating that he make a north-south run on the buildings – parallel to a line of Marine Humvees – with his cannon .

'Once we verified that the Air Force pilot had the correct area in his sights, we crossed behind him as he was lining up for his attack run to make certain that he was pointed at the correct group of buildings, before handing final clearance control back to the Marines on the ground. With the friendly troops so close to the buildings, it was better that they had the final say that he wasn't pointed at them if at all possible. The A-10 pilot walked a line of 30 mm rounds right down the top of the buildings from which the Marines were receiving the majority of the fire. That enabled them to effectively break contact and move back toward the bridge, and away from the mosque complex. Both A-10s then headed off-station as they had hit bingo fuel state.

'An M1A2 Abrams main battle tank then moved up and sat across from the complex in the position where the Marine convoy had initially been located. After a few minutes, additional fire was directed at the M1A2 from a building opposite the mosque. The tank crew replied in kind, firing a single round into the building in an effort to silence the fires in that area, before moving back towards the bridge.

'At this point the ground FAC relayed to us that he and his troops were no longer taking fire, and that he was going to call in some artillery while they regrouped, before attempting to enter the mosque complex once again.

'We decided to make a quick run to the tanker at this point, topping off for maximum on-station time. As we headed to the tanker, we were able to relay some comms to the FAC from several medevac helicopters that were out of radio range as they approached the convoy at low level. We also asked the DASC to send additional CAS assets to help support the convoy. We specifically requested attack helicopter assets, which would have been especially useful in the urban terrain due the nature of the close-in fighting. We quickly topped off our tanks and returned to the convoy's location, monitoring the unit's radio frequency all the way in.

'By the time we had re-established ourselves on-station over central Baghdad, the convoy had regrouped after the initial attack, pushed down the road past the mosque complex and was now flanked by a series of buildings to their right on the south side of the road. The Marines had received additional fire from these buildings and had now stopped a safe distance away. Not wanting to trade fire with a well-entrenched enemy, the Marines instructed us to take out the buildings from which they had been shot at.

'We followed the talk-on by the ground FAC and made a dry run to confirm his position, and the exact building that he wanted attacked. The Marines were right on the edge of the acceptable distance for us to put down a 500-lb LGB, so we told them to prepare for the pass, and get everyone's heads down. We delivered a delayed-fused LGB into the last building on the block as instructed and then set up to the west for another attack. The ground control indicated a direct hit, and instructed us to walk our next LGBs one building toward the west, closer to their position. We made two more runs, delivering one bomb each time and walking them down the line of buildings where the convoy had received fire. After we were "Winchester" (out of ordnance), there was one additional building that the ground controller wanted taken out that was across the street from the original building that we had bombed.

'A section of RAF Tornado GR 4s had by now checked in on-station, loaded with 1000-lb Enhanced Paveway II LGBs. While we were familiar with the target area, the RAF crews were not certain which buildings in the area we were targeting. Several buildings had been damaged from the initial A-10 and M1A2 attacks, and we wanted to ensure that the Tornado crews didn't drop their ordnance too close to the friendly forces.

'The Raytheon-developed Enhanced Paveway II carried by these jets was an outstanding weapon for a CAS aircraft, and it was employed exclusively by the RAF in OIF. The bomb combined the strengths of both the LGB and JDAM, as they could be used as a traditional laser-guided weapon, with pinpoint accuracy, or they could be dropped using accurate coordinates and GPS guidance thanks to the Enhanced Paveway's Global Positioning System Aided Inertial Navigation System, or GAINS for short. Often in OIF, US TACAIR aircraft would find themselves loaded out with LGBs on poor weather days, which rendered the weapons useless, or outfitted with JDAM and unable to derive accurate coordinates from ground FACs which achieved the level of accuracy dictated by the campaign's strict RoE. The Enhanced Paveway offered you the best of both worlds in one package.

'We had the LTS generate accurate coordinates for the Tornado GR 4s using the software embedded in the guidance pod which allowed precise coordinate generation for GPS munitions. Having passed the target coordinates to the British crew, we watched as the lead aircraft set itself up for an attack run. After clearing him "hot", we lased the target on the pre-coordinated code, allowing the Enhanced Paveway to transition from GPS to laser guidance and score a direct hit. This technique not only minimised the time required for a talk-on, it also ensured accurate bomb delivery, as the FAC(A) familiar with the target got to guide the ordnance in its terminal phase.

'Bullet 100' was the last of VF-2's ten aircraft to receive its scoreboard of 49 LGBs and ten JDAM silhouettes. Indeed, the squadron's maintainers only applied the mission tally 24 hours prior to the unit departing CV-64 for Oceana on 31 May 2003. Befitting its status as the 'Bounty Hunters'' colour jet, BuNo 163894 dropped more bombs than any other Tomcat in VF-2 during OIF (*PH2 Dan McLain*)

Proudly displaying its bomb tally, 'Bullet 106' (BuNo 164342) taxis towards one of CV-64's bow catapults on 15 April 2003. 'Connie' departed the NAG 48 hours later (*PH2 Dan McLain*)

'The ground FAC was impressed by the difference between a 500-lb and 1000-lb bomb. After surveying the area, he got on the radio and told us that all enemy fire had been silenced, and that they were going to push further down the road. He finished by thanking us for our support.

'Before checking out, we handed control of the area over to a section of Marine AH-1Ws that had responded to our request to the DASC for rotary wing assets. After a quick situation report, we checked out and they continued to cover the convoy as it pushed further east of the river into the heart of Baghdad.'

MARINE SUPPORT

VF-31 also had its fair share of talented FAC(A) crews within its midst, and they too proved a great help to troops on the ground. Heading up CVW-14's commitment to expeditionary warfare in OIF was 'Tomcatters' RIO Lt Cdr John Patterson, who was chosen pre-war by his CAG, Capt Casey Albright, to be the air wing's CAS subject matter expert. Few boasted better qualifications for the job, with Patterson having performed the role of strike leader in OEF and OSW for both CVW-7 and -14. He had also served as a Strike Fighter Tactics Instructor, a Marine Corps Aviation Weapons and Tactics Instructor, FAC(A) Instructor and Night Vision Device Instructor.

Patterson's primary mission in the weeks leading up to OIF was to ensure that CVW-14's TACAIR crews were ready to provide the most effective CAS possible right from the start of the land war. To achieve this, he worked closely with ground FACs from the Army's V Corps during exercises in the Kuwaiti desert. Patterson also represented CVW-14 in an emergency planning cell established by the 1st MEF that included the 3rd Marine Air Wing (the primary CAS asset supporting the Marines in OIF) and FAC(A)s and Airborne Command and Control representatives from CVW-2 and -5.

According to VF-31's XO, Cdr Aaron Cudnohufsky;

'The cell initiated command and control and CAS allocation procedures for naval TACAIR which greatly increased the efficient flow of sorties in support of US Marines. As the direct result of these efforts, naval TACAIR was able to compensate for a shortage of Marine direct support assets, funnelling excess armed reconnaissance and SCAR sorties

Lt Cdr John Patterson was one of the most highly qualified RIOs to see action in OIF with VF-31, and he was chosen to be CVW-14's CAS subject matter expert pre-war as a result. He also helped the 'Tomcatters' hastily get to grips with JDAM following the installation of D04 into the unit's F-14Ds in late February 2003, having had previous experience with the weapon when serving with CVW-7 in OEF in 2001-02 (*VF-31*)

The availability of S-3 tankers over the carriers in the NAG proved crucial on a near-daily basis for the F/A-18 community, but less so for the 'longer-legged' F-14s. Nevertheless, it was always comforting to know that spare gas was available should a jet arrive in the overhead a little low on fuel. Conversely, as in this case, crews could top off their tanks following take-off, prior to heading north into Iraq via a 'big wing tanker'. Here, LGB-toting 'Tomcatter 102' (BuNo 163904) moves in on VS-35's S-3B BuNo 159763 (*Lt Cdr Jim Muse*)

to ensure the destruction of the Iraqi Army's IV Corps, effectively securing the critical, but lightly defended, supply lines of the 1st MEF in their advance on Baghdad. So effective were these efforts that they led to a 100 per cent elimination of the combat capability of the Iraqi IV Corps through destruction and desertion, allowing Marine ground forces to later capture IV Corps headquarters in Al Amarah without having to fire a shot. Moreover, Lt Cdr Patterson also personally participated in this destruction, conceiving, planning and leading a CVW-14 strike package to destroy IV Corps' artillery regimental headquarters.

'This sortie was just one of thirteen missions that Lt Cdr Patterson flew in OIF as a Strike Leader and FAC(A), during which he personally expended 23 LGB, GPS and general purpose bombs, as well as 500 rounds of 20 mm cannon fire against enemy forces, including multiple instances in support of friendly forces in direct contact with the enemy. In one particularly memorable mission flown on 30 March, Patterson acted as the FAC(A) for his section, which duly destroyed enemy armour and artillery that had damaged three Apache helicopters and halted the V Corps advance south of Al Hillah. Throughout this mission, Patterson and his pilot remained on-station over the target area despite the presence of enemy AAA and SAM batteries.'

Due to the complexity of the FAC(A) mission, the Navy would only allow suitably qualified two-man crews to undertake such sorties. There were only a handful of FAC(A)s in-theatre, so in order to keep the battlefield serviced, SCAR and armed reconnaissance missions came to prominence early on in the campaign. Both could be performed by virtually any Tomcat crew operating in a two-aircraft section, as VF-2's Cdr Denneny explained;

'When given a SCAR or armed reconnaissance mission, we would be allocated a certain area to work over by a controlling body in-theatre in the knowledge that there were no friendlies in that kill box. We had been authorised to drop our weapons against targets of opportunity, and once we had spotted perhaps an aircraft or a tank on the ground, we would call our controller, who confirmed that we were cleared to release our bombs.

'SCAR and armed reconnaissance missions allowed virtually any aircraft in CVW-2 that was capable of carrying ordnance to become a viable attack platform, as long as the threat environment was deemed to be benign and the collateral damage issues were negligible.

'VF-2's load-out of choice for SCAR and armed reconnaissance was four 500-lb LGBs. We could head into Iraq and offer good support for the guys on the ground with such a bomb fit, but if there were no targets to hit, I could return to the ship with all my ordnance in place, as the F-14 in this configuration was fully recoverable.'

Although often kept busy in his role as a FAC(A), VF-2's Lt Cdr Michael Peterson also participated in a number of impromptu SCAR and armed reconnaissance missions;

'Upon checking in with "Warhawk" one day as a FAC(A), my section was reassigned to check in with a ground unit that had some work for us. We headed to the assigned Kill Box Keypad location and checked in with the ground unit's FAC, notifying him that we had three 500-lb GBU-12 LGBs apiece, and about 40 minutes of on-station time. The FAC passed us his location in grid coordinates on a secure radio.

'We much preferred working in the six- or eight-digit Military Grid Reference System after having modifications carried out to the software and LTS used by our F-14Ds. Not only was it the standard system used by the ground units, the grid coordinates also made it very easy for us to locate friendly forces, or enemy targets, on the 1:50,000 charts that we carried in the cockpit. Additionally, when we found targets with our LTS, we could accurately produce the grid location of the targets so that the ground FAC could quickly cross-reference the location and confirm that there were no friendly units operating in that area.

'We headed to the coordinates passed and located a convoy exhibiting Coalition identification markings travelling north on a major road. The ground controller verified that this was his convoy, and that he wanted us to scout along the Lines of Communication (roads) ahead of his convoy to look for possible ambush locations or resistance as they pushed north.

'In true armed reconnaissance fashion, my wingman and I headed north, searching visually and with the LTS. We came upon a compound about nine kilometres up the road that was filled with revetments, some of which contained military vehicles. We passed the coordinates and a description of the target to the convoy FAC, and he stated that it was an Iraqi military compound. He also told us that it was where the convoy was headed as part of its mission to secure the area on the way north.

'Upon the direction of the ground FAC, we made multiple passes and took out four revetted vehicles, including one tank, prior to the convoy pushing into the area. While the compound was being secured by the troops on the ground, we continued north and found additional revetted vehicles in another compound further up the road. After checking with the ground controller once again, we expended our remaining ordnance on these vehicles prior to the convoy securing this area too.

'This mission, while relatively uneventful from our perspective, was typical of the myriad armed reconnaissance sorties flown in support of the rapid ground advance to the north by V Corps and the 1st MEF, where potential ground resistance was minimised through the effective use of tactical aircraft.'

GO FOR YOUR GUN

Like their Hornet brethren in OIF, Tomcat crews viewed their internally mounted M61 Vulcan 20 mm cannon as a weapon of last resort should the enemy still be in contact with friendlies on the ground once the F-14 had exhausted all of its bombs. On 30 March, while supporting the stalled V Corps advance in southern Iraq, a VF-2 section had cause to strafe. This was the first time that a Tomcat crew from CV-64 had fired their cannon in OIF. Leading the section were Lt Tony Culic and his RIO, and mission commander, CVW-2 DCAG Capt Craig Geron. The latter recalled;

'We were flying a night CAS sortie in marginal weather between An Nasiriyah and An Najaf. An Army FAC on the ground, who was operating with troops heading northwest towards An Najaf, asked my section of Tomcats to take out some Iraqi soldiers who were firing at them from behind a large fence, backed by a treeline. I could tell the guys on the ground really needed our support, so I made the decision to lead my section down through the layers of cloud that blanketed the area so that we could employ out LGBs against the enemy.

'Once overhead, and having been bracketed by AAA, I quickly ascertained the tactical picture below us and directed a series of LGB runs on both the Iraqi troops and a nearby APC. Despite both Tomcats dropping two LGBs apiece on the targets, the FAC told us that they were still being fired upon, and he asked us could we strafe?

'Carrying plenty of gas, we decided that it was a benign threat environment as there appeared to be no SAMs. There were no other TACAIR types or attack helicopters available to carry out this request, so after descending still further, we prepared to strafe the enemy positions.

His F-14D (BuNo 164342) still stained by the cordite deposits left by the rounds fired from its M61 Vulcan 20 mm cannon, Lt Tony Culic poses for the camera after becoming VF-2's first strafer in OIF on the night of 30 March 2003. He received an Air Medal for actions, the citation for which read, in part, as follows;

'He led his flight below the cloud layers to successfully destroy an Iraqi APC hiding in a treeline. After refuelling, and despite deteriorating weather, he once again led his flight below the clouds and into a high threat area to conduct attacks in support of Coalition troops who were being fired upon. He quickly and skilfully directed multiple visual bomb and gun attacks at very high speed and low altitude, destroying or dispersing all enemy forces and rescuing Coalition troops' (*PH2 Dan McLain*)

'Our primary concern during our gunnery passes was the fact that we were now well within the range of MANPADS. Nevertheless, we positioned ourselves for the strafing runs just under the overcast, which started at around 8000 ft, and conducted a modified strafing pattern that bottomed out at 2500 ft. Obviously, we could not achieve pinpoint accuracy when strafing at night, so these passes were more "fire for effect". However, we got the Iraqis to put their heads down, and convinced them that the soldiers they were firing on had robust aerial support.'

Geron, Culic and their wingmen were awarded Air Medals following the success of this mission.

The dropping of 'dumb' bombs from an F-14 was almost as rare an occurrence as the employment of the cannon in OIF, although two crews from VF-2 enjoyed spectacular results with four 500-lb Mk 82 'slicks' on 27 March. The RIO in one of the jets was Lt(jg) Pat Baker;

'We had been conducting a standard TARPS mission along the Euphrates River, looking at two or three air defence sites, as well as a possible command and control facility that our intelligence folks thought was in the area They needed photos of the latter in order to confirm its purpose for target assignment. What was different for us that day was the fact that the ATO gave us two jets armed with a pair of Mk 82 bombs apiece. This was the first time VF-2 had carried such a mixed load, featuring both bombs and a TARPS pod. This allowed us to act as a stop gap bomber should anyone need immediate on-call support while we were over southern Iraq.

'I was in the back seat of the Dash 2 jet, leaving the RIO in the lead aircraft to run the flight in terms of coordinating the navigation for all the photo-run targets. My job was to work the radios for my pilot, Lt Sean Mathieson, checking with AWACS controllers and FACs on

VF-2's unique bomb-armed TARPS jet configuration (*PH2 Dan McLain*)

the ground as to whether anyone needed our bombs. Having
bounced around through a series of
different nets on various frequencies, I ended up talking to a British
Army FAC near Basra. He wanted
us to head down the Shatt al-Arab
waterway and attack Saddam's
presidential yacht, which had been
hit by a Maverick fired from an
S-3B two days earlier and then
missed by two LGB-toting F/A-18s.
By the time I contacted the FAC, we
had finished our reconnaissance
runs and were about to head south
over the NAG to hit the tanker and
then head back to the carrier.

'The FAC was not actually near the yacht, so he was relaying
information that he had recently received to us when he was describing
where the vessel was situated. We were at high altitude, scouring the port
facility through binoculars looking for the yacht. We spotted the burnt-
out warehouses that had been hit in error by the F/A-18s the previous day,
and these served as a marker for the yacht. It was moored between two
freighters, with a third half-sunken vessel nearby. The Maverick damage
was clearly visible, with smoke rising from the vessel's superstructure.

'The lead jet, flown by Lt Mark Callari and Lt(jg) Jeff Sims (RIO),
rolled in first, while we provided high cover for it – we were not sure of the
AAA or SAM threats in the area. Their first bomb hit the bow, and
having been unopposed in the attack, they came in and dropped the
second, which struck the vessel just forward of amidships.

'The lead jet then swapped places with us, Lt Mathieson following his
CCIP (Continuously Computed Impact Point) crosshairs in the HUD,
which were centred on the vessel. We dropped both of our bombs in the
same attack, one hitting the hull just above the waterline and the other
disappearing amongst the yacht's superstructure. When we left the target
the ship was on fire, although we knew we had not inflicted sufficient
damage to sink it as we were carrying the wrong type of ordnance.
Assuming that we were going to be supporting ground troops, we had had
our Mk 82s fitted with instantaneous fuses. Therefore, the weapons
exploded as soon as they came into contact with the ship, rather than
burying themselves into the heart of the vessel before detonating.

'I never got to see my bombs hitting home in all the LGB and JDAM
missions that we flew in OIF. However, on this occasion, thanks to the
diving, rolling and pulling off of the target that we had had to do in order
to accurately deliver our Mk 82s, I was able to see the two little grey
"blurs" that were our bombs hitting the ship as I peered back over my
shoulder at the target.'

OP TEMPO

All three Tomcat units in the NAG were kept incredibly busy throughout
the conflict, flying a record number of sorties during the 30 days that

Lt(jg) Pat Baker and Lt Sean
Mathieson pose with their bombed
up TARPS jet (BuNo 164350) the day
after attacking Saddam Hussein's
presidential yacht on 17 March 2003.
Pilot Mathieson recalled;

'As the needs for CAS grew in OIF,
it became standard to load Mk 82
500-lb "dumb" bombs on all the
TARPS jets. These flights were also
dubbed the "chum" flights, in that
we flew as low as our Special
Instructions permitted to gain the
highest resolution on the imagery.
Low, straight and level was not
where we wanted to be in an
increasingly hostile SAM/AAA-rich
environment, however.

'After imaging over two-dozen
targets, we checked in with AWACS
to see if there was any additional
tasking. We were immediately sent
down the Shatt al-Arab waterway to
Basra, where a ground FAC needed
ordnance on the presidential yacht.
Previous strikes had crippled the
large vessel, and we were being
called in to finish the job off. I flew
high cover, keeping my lead in sight
as he rolled in on the large, white
vessel. Having expended his
ordnance, I descended to our
pre-planned dive altitude and rolled
in on the target. Both of my 500-lb
bombs struck the hull of the yacht,
cascading into a large fireball below
us. Mission completed, we headed
back to the "Connie" for two OK
3-wire landings' (*PH2 Dan McLain*)

constituted the air-strike phase of OIF. Prior to that, both VF-2 and VF-31 had also maintained a punishing sortie tempo in support of OSW. Whilst operating under Fifth Fleet control during OSW/OIF, VF-2 had flown 483 sorties and dropped 294 LGBs/JDAM/Mk 82 bombs, VF-31 had completed 585 sorties and dropped 239 LGBs/JDAM/Mk 82 bombs, and VF-154 (whose operations are detailed in the next chapter) had flown a staggering 1006 sorties and dropped 358 LGBs.

To sustain this operational tempo, the squadrons needed their maintenance departments to keep at least four to six of their ten (or twelve, in VF-154's case) jets airworthy and up on the flightdeck at the start of each day's flying. Achieving this number of serviceable aircraft was crucial, as the Tomcat was usually the cornerstone around which the air wing built its daily mission cycles due to the jet's myriad capabilities. Capt Craig Geron explained how this worked;

'There were fixed time limits for air wing mission cycles, based on the distance that you flew and the fuel that was available – CV-64 was located the furthest south of the three NAG carriers, so gas was always a major factor for us. The CAOC had worked out the distribution of waves that we flew using these limits. Typically, we would fly three to four waves during our flight period, with the first and third waves being heavy on jets and the second and fourth being lighter.

'When working out the composition of these waves, we tried to make sure that we did not overload the contribution of the F-14s. You could usually count on having a division of four jets available at the start of every day. You would frontload the flying schedule after a day's worth of maintenance with the four available Tomcats, hopefully having a fifth as a spare. You would then reduce the requirements for the F-14 in the later waves. From a management standpoint, you made your waves up around the availability of the F-14s, with four going in the first launch, followed by two more on each subsequent cycle.

'A variation on this theme was to double cycle the Tomcats, leaving them airborne to complete two back-to-back missions, and thus avoid a turnaround on the deck. Once the jet was in the air it did well, but the challenge was getting the Tomcat flying – VF-2 was spending between 60 and 70 maintenance hours per flying hour in an effort to keep its aircraft mission ready.

'We were fully aware pre-war that the F-14s would require more work to keep them in the air. The success story was that we had the parts

Named *Al Mansur* (The Victor), Saddam Hussein's presidential yacht had been one of the world's largest and most impressive vessels of its kind prior to it appearing on the CAOC's ATO. Eight decks high and 350 feet long, the Finnish-built ship weighed 7359 tons and looked more like a cross-channel ferry than a private boat. It boasted five expansive state cabins for Saddam and his family, and there was even a secret escape route leading from the president's room to a submarine pod. Launched in 1982, it was the largest vessel in the Iraqi Navy, but it had no military use. The ship was designed to Saddam's specifications and decorated in marble and exotic woods with silver and gold fittings. Permanently staffed by 120 Special Republican Guard troops, the vessel was moved from the port of Umm Qasr to Basra just days before the war began in an effort to afford it better protection – the order for the move was issued directly by Saddam himself. The *Al Mansur* had been targeted for destruction because the CAOC had received reports that the vessel's extensive radio suite was being used for battlefield communications (*Daily Mirror*)

F-14D BuNo 164344 provides the backdrop for this group shot of VF-31's officer cadre on the very day that CVN-72 chopped out of the NAG – 7 April 2003. The squadron's ten F-14Ds had flown 585 sorties totalling 1744 combat hours during OIF. 'Tomcatter 103' dropped 34 LGB/JDAM during the campaign, and was also involved in ground strafing. Delivered to the Navy on 11 October 1991, the aircraft was initially flown by VF-124 at Miramar until passed on to VF-31 in 1992 when the latter unit replaced its F-14As with D-model Tomcats. It remained with the 'Tomcatters' until transferred to VF-2 in 1999, BuNo 164344 returning to VF-31 two years later. Having survived OIF, the aircraft was written off when it crashed into the Pacific Ocean two miles west of Point Loma, California, on the morning of 29 March 2004. Its crew had experienced fuel transfer problems soon after launching from USS *John C Stennis* (CVN-74) on a routine training mission off San Diego during CVW-14's pre-cruise work-ups. Pilot Lt Dan Komar and RIO Lt(jg) Matt Janczak attempted to fly the jet back to nearby NAS North Island and carry out an emergency landing, but the F-14 ran out of fuel and the crew ejected three miles south of the base. Both men were soon rescued and the wreckage of the jet was later recovered (*VF-31*)

available in-theatre to allow these veteran aircraft to remain serviceable, despite having seven carriers deployed. Indeed, the only F-14Ds that were not in-theatre during OIF were four jets kept back with the fleet replacement squadron at NAS Oceana and two test aircraft with VX-30 at NAWC China Lake.

'Thanks to superb spares support and well-trained maintenance personnel, the Tomcat and the LTS enjoyed excellent reliability in OIF. Indeed, VF-2's performance in terms of maintenance and reliability was better in combat than it had been on previous CVW-2 OSW cruises when it had operated as the only F-14 unit in the NAG. Quite simply, OIF was a Tomcat success story.'

VF-2's Lt Cdr Mike Peterson was also fulsome in his praise for the maintainers that kept the F-14s in the air during the campaign;

'The Navy only had three F-14D units, and this was the first and last time that all of them were deployed at once. It was a credit to the maintenance crews of these squadrons, and the personnel back at the Fighter Wing at NAS Oceana, that we could keep all these assets combat ready given the limited, and highly tasked, parts supply train that they had to maintain. All the good work that we did as aircrew during the war started with our maintainers. In some ways, it was on their backs that the heaviest burden fell. My missions lasted four to eight hours, but our troops worked 12- to 18-hour days throughout the entire war.'

CVN-72 was relieved in-theatre by USS *Nimitz* (CVN-68) on 7 April 2003, and in a portent of things to come, the latter carrier's embarked air wing (CVW-11) was devoid of Tomcats. *Abraham Lincoln* had also bade farewell to its F-14s by the time President George W Bush flew aboard on 1 May to declare that major hostilities were over in Iraq. VF-31 had departed for NAS Oceana 24 hours earlier, thus signalling the end of the unit's marathon 286-day deployment. Both CV-63 and CV-64 pulled out of the Arabian Gulf on 17 April, and by 1 June all three NAG-based Tomcat squadrons had returned home.

'BLACK KNIGHTS'

VF-154's war was undoubtedly the most unusual of any of the Tomcat units committed to OIF. Deployed on its final cruise with the F-14A as part of CVW-5, the 'Black Knights' arrived on station in the far north of the NAG aboard *Kitty Hawk* on 26 February 2003. Chosen to be the dedicated CAS air wing by the CAOC, CVW-5 had not operated in this region since July 1999. Despite its unfamiliarity with current procedures in OSW, VF-154 completed a handful of successful CAS and FAC(A) missions in southern and western Iraq in the three weeks leading up to OIF.

Prior to the squadron's spring deployment, VF-154 had tailored its training to maximise its precision strike capabilities, including dedicated training in target acquisition in urban environments. During CVW-5 work-ups, the unit was directly responsible for developing standardised precision FAC(A) and CAS tactics for the entire air wing.

Once in-theatre, VF-154's pre-deployment focus on the air-to-ground mission allowed it to work with many different assets as CVW-5 looked to expand its role both in Expeditionary Warfare and precision CAS in the combat environment. After short notice tasking from CENTCOM, VF-154 detached four crews (augmented by FAC(A) instructors recently drafted in from NSAWC) and four jets to Al Udeid air base, in Qatar. With combat operations looming, these crews quickly scheduled multiple training events to teach SCAR to the inter-Coalition and inter-service assets based at Al Udeid. Whilst ashore, VF-154 worked closely with RAF Tornado GR 4s, USAF F-15Es, F-16CGs and F-16CJs and Royal Australian Air Force (RAAF) F/A-18As.

This training evolution subsequently paid huge dividends, as VF-154 crews directly controlled laser-guided munitions and passed LTS target coordinates for the successful employment of British Enhanced Paveway II/III LGBs, standard LGBs and JDAM dropped from Coalition aircraft. The Al Udeid training detachment also helped maximise the lethality of supported ground forces by reducing the time between precision weapons impacts down to the NSAWC recommendation of one bomb per minute for over 20 minutes, and less in the case of GPS-guided munitions.

The success of the Al Udeid operation pre-war can be gauged by the fact that CENTCOM contacted CVW-5 directly on the eve of OIF and requested that VF-154 send a third of its assets to Qatar to support Coalition land-based aircraft and SOF squads operating inside Iraq. The

Still carrying its GBU-12s, 'Nite 103' (BuNo 161293) joins the recovery pattern overhead CV-63 in early March 2003. This particular aircraft ended OIF as the high-time ordnance expender, its crews delivery no fewer than 51 LGBs on targets during the campaign. Delivered to the Navy in late 1981 and issued to Miramar-based VF-2, BuNo 161293 completed three *WestPacs* with the unit as part of CVW-2 before being transferred to VF-21 in late 1988. After a further two *WestPacs* with the 'Freelancers' (part of CVW-14), the aircraft was left behind at Miramar when VF-21 transferred to Japan in August 1991 to join CVW-5. It was passed on to CVW-15's VF-111 upon the latter unit's return from its 1991 *WestPac* in December of that year, and the jet remained with the 'Sundowners' until the unit's disestablishment on 31 March 1995. The fighter then served with VF-101 at Oceana, prior to being overhauled at NAS Jacksonville in early 1998 and transferred to CVW-5's VF-154 at NAF Atsugi, Japan. The jet remained with the 'Black Knights' in Japan until it accompanied the unit back to Oceana on 24 September 2003. Like the rest of VF-154's F-14As, it was duly stricken from the inventory (on 16 December 2003) (*VF-154*) unit's XO, Cdr Doug Waters, was ashore at the time when he received word of CENTCOM's unusual request. He recalled;

'I was an LNO (liaison officer) with the CAOC at Prince Sultan air base ("PSAB") during the weeks prior to the war. My job was to scrub the OPLAN for OIF from a Navy viewpoint, basically make sure that the requested sortie numbers, ordnance loads and tankers would work for carrier-based fighters, and their planned cycle times.

'While working the OPLAN scrub, I began to hear that there were moves afoot to bring additional FAC(A)-capable Tomcats and crews out to work directly with Coalition ground forces. At first it sounded like additional aircraft – rumoured to be F-14Bs from VF-11 and VF-143 – would be added to one of the carriers (probably CV-64) already in-theatre, then it became apparent that the plan would involve basing jets ashore. Some in the Navy didn't like the idea of putting carrier-based aircraft ashore – I guess they felt it was an admission that the Air Force had the better idea. I felt just the opposite, for I thought that it showed the inherent flexibility of carrier-based fighters. We could operate from either venue if required, which is obviously not true for land-based fighters.

'I was soon told that it was my squadron that was going to support this plan. I would subsequently find out that VF-154 was picked for this role because of the high serviceability rates that we had achieved with our veteran F-14As – the highest for TACAIR in-theatre. Since the squadron CO, Cdr James Flatley, was a FAC(A), and would be leading the detachment ashore, I needed to get back to VF-154. When I stepped back on the deck of CV-63 three-and-a-half weeks after flying off on the transit over from Japan, I remember thinking thank God I was out of "PSAB" and back with my unit where I belonged.'

WAR ASHORE

Five aircraft and five crews were duly put ashore on the eve of OIF, VF-154's CO, three department heads, its training officer and several augment instructors from NSAWC being charged with the responsibility of waging the impending war from Al Udeid. The unit's maintenance section came up with a novel plan to keep its elderly charges serviceable whilst ashore, as Cdr Waters explained;

'Their plan was simple, yet effective – take the minimum number of maintainers possible ashore so that the squadron would not be precluded from maintaining a high ship-based operational tempo in support of normal ATO tasking. They did this by handpicking the maintainers sent to Qatar, and then worked informal relationships with existing units already there in order to garner external support for the detachment.

'The 30 maintainers would work closely with both the RAAF Hornet detachment and the 157th Fighter Squadron (FS), South Carolina Air National Guard, which flew F-16CJs. Both units were exceptionally helpful, and without the liaison set up between them and the "Black Knights", it would have been very difficult to achieve the 100 per cent combat sortie completion rate that was maintained while operating out of Qatar. The Aussies were able to use their composite shop to aid in any airframe/metalworking issues that came up for our aircraft, and they also fashioned an adapter that allowed us to use existing USAF servicing equipment to replenish the nitrogen bottles used to cool our AIM-9Ms.

VF-154's Al Udeid det pose for a group shot on the flightline in late March 2003. The naval aviator standing at the extreme left in the rear row is NSAWC augmentee Lt Cdr Scotty McDonald, who was forced to eject from his Tomcat over Iraq several days after this photograph was taken. Providing the backdrop to this shot is 'Nite 112' (BuNo 158624), which dropped 28 LGBs in OIF (VF-154)

A division of four Qatar det F-14As prepare to taxi out for a dusk mission at Al Udeid in early April 2003. Behind them can be seen F-16CJs from the USAF's 389th FS, as well as RAAF F/A-18As from No 75 Sqn and RAF Tornado GR 4s. The VF-154 crews got to work closely with all three types, as well as the co-located F-15Es of the 4th FW. 'Nite 110' (BuNo 161288) expended 35 LGBs, which made it the most prolific of the five shore-based Tomcats in terms of ordnance dropped in OIF (VF-154)

'The South Carolina Guard guys helped the detachment gain access to the support equipment it required, and they went out of their way to make sure our troops were well taken care of while in Qatar. Suffice it to say, without the Aussies and the Air Guard guys basically "adopting" our maintainers, we would have had to bring more personnel ashore, with negative implications to the unit's ability to generate ATO sorties from CV-63.'

Once OIF started, the benefits of having VF-154's cadre of FAC(A)s in Qatar soon became apparent. They were able to brief, debrief and operate on a continuing basis with the air assets that they would control over Iraq, face-to-face liaison making the entire strike package much more efficient and lethal. The unit's work with the 4th Fighter Wing's 335th and 336th FSs was particularly successful, with the pairing of the F-14A and F-15E proving deadly when conducting TCT/TF-20 missions in support of SOF.

A VF-154 RIO who was one of the FAC(A)-qualified naval aviators chosen to fly from Qatar provided the Author with the following account of a mission he participated in from Al Udeid on 3 April;

'It was supposed to be a six-hour "Black Knight" division FAC(A) flight in support of ground forces. Three hours prior to take-off, we received our intelligence update, and then briefed with our strike assets. Tonight, we'd have four F-15Es and two F-16CJs as our primary strikers. Three weeks of briefing with the same guys made for an expeditious proceeding. After the brief, we geared up and piled into the minivan for the drive to the flightline – while minivans may be good for "soccer mums", they're not very accommodating for eight fully dressed aviators.

'Ten minutes later we arrived on the flightline and quickly read the Aircraft Discrepancy Books. We'd been flying the same jets for the last three weeks, so we only gave the books a cursory glance. We then grabbed a few bottles of water and walked to the aircraft. After start-up we taxied out to the runway, each jet armed with four GBU-12 LGBs apiece. One of the cool things about taking off from Qatar was the requirement to be above 15,000 ft (thus negating the MANPAD threat) prior to actually leaving the airfield boundaries! Two minutes after the first of our F-14s had rolled, we had all joined up at 23,000 ft and proceeded feet wet over the NAG on our way to Iraq.

'An hour later the sun had completely set, we had finished our first airborne refuelling and we were proceeding west in search of our next tanker. Within 30 minutes all four F-14 crews had topped off for the second time and were finally ready to check in with our controlling agency. The latter informed us that we were still on schedule, and that the ground forces were waiting for us in central Iraq. For the purpose of continuity, we split into two sections so that we could constantly have eyes in the target area while the other section refuelled.

'As the first section worked its way towards the specific element that we were supporting, it became apparent that the friendlies on the ground had taken some casualties from a car bomb that had been set off. Our first mission of the night would be to sanitise the area of any threats so we could medevac out the casualties. After reconnoitring the area, the lead section discovered a hostile vehicle driving towards the landing zone and eliminated it with a GBU-12. They then proceeded to fly high cover for the medevac helicopter, escorting it back to friendly forces.

'The second "Black Knight" section then arrived on scene and proceeded to protect the ground forces from any threat proceeding from the lake side of the nearby Hadditha Dam, on which the friendlies had set up their defensive position. We were very concerned that the Iraqis would attempt to breach the dam in an attempt to flood the Euphrates River which ran through the valley below it, as well as Karbala to the south.

'Right about then we were fired on by several AAA pieces from southwest of the dam. Using NVGs, and slaving the FLIR to the HUD, we were able to roll in on the AAA and destroy a weapon with an LGB. Wanting to save some of our ordnance for follow on "pop up" threats, we called in two F-15Es and guided their LGBs onto adjacent AAA pieces.

'At about this time the lead section arrived back on scene, and after a FAC-to-FAC turnover, they relieved us. We then got word from our buddies on the ground that one of their reconnaissance units had discovered more AAA pieces at an airfield five kilometres south of the dam. They asked us to check it out, and after some searching, we were able to find about ten S-60 AAA weapons dispersed around the airfield. After dropping one LGB to mark the target for our USAF brethren, we turned the remainder over for them to destroy. Now reaching bingo fuel,

Bombs gone, 'Nite 102' (BuNo 161280) is now just minutes away from landing back aboard CV-63. *Kitty Hawk* was positioned furthest north of the three carriers in the NAG, which meant that CVW-5's TACAIR jets enjoyed the shortest mission transit times of all the sea-based naval aircraft operating in the south. BuNo 161280 ended the campaign with 35 LGB silhouettes beneath its cockpit. Delivered new to VF-101 on 22 August 1981, this TARPS-capable aircraft subsequently served with VF-31, VF-103, VF-102 (with whom it saw action in *Desert Storm*) and VF-101 once again, before being transferred to VF-154 in early 1998. Following its return to Oceana in September 2003, BuNo 161280 was stricken on 6 October that same year (*VF-154*)

'Nite 111' (BuNo 161292) receives fuel from a 9th Air Refueling Squadron KC-10A, flying out of Al Dhafra air base, in the United Arab Emirates. VF-154's Al Udeid jets always hit a 'big wing' tanker prior to pressing into Iraq, this initial refuelling usually taking place at dusk (*VF-154*)

the lead section headed for the tanker, and then home, as the second section arrived back on scene.

'I don't know if the Iraqis to the southwest of the dam thought we had left or not, but they started shooting AAA at it soon after the lead section departed. Quickly finding the AAA piece on NVGs and FLIR, we passed two sets of coordinates to a section of F-16s and told them to put a JDAM on each of them. We orbited overhead and watched on our FLIR as both JDAM shacked their intended targets. Having destroyed the remaining AAA pieces to the southwest, we passed off the FAC(A) roll to a section of A-10s and headed south to find our second to last tanker of the night.

'Unfortunately the weather was now starting to roll in, and after some attempts to get the tanker to clear air, we finally gave up and rendezvoused in the "goo". Our wingman, being lower on fuel, would tank first. Just as he was plugging in, he had an engine compressor stall and disappeared into the darkness below. Not having a lot of fuel, or time, to play with, we decided to tank while he rejoined. After a couple of minutes, and some radio calls, he magically appeared off our right wing. His engine then stalled again, and in the ensuing melee I watched him cross-planform directly in front of the tanker – I instinctively ducked, waiting for the ensuing fireball that would kill us all. Fortunately, he just missed the tanker and disappeared down our left side back into the darkness. I can honestly say that was the scariest moment of my life.

'Tragedy averted, we managed to finish refuelling our section and then headed back east towards our last tanker. After completing our final tanking evolution, we flew back out over the Gulf, turned south and tracked down the aerial highway to Qatar. Forty minutes later we checked in with Base Ops to ascertain the status of the field. Base Ops replied that they were in the middle of a huge sandstorm, and that we could try to shoot the approach or divert to a different base. We decided that we had enough fuel to try to get down at Qatar and divert if we couldn't land.

'Surprisingly, we were able to see the field at 15 miles and set up for individual straight-in approaches. We could see the runway clear as day until we lost sight of everything when we flew into the sandstorm at a height of just 100 ft above the ground. Our wingman, one mile in trail, immediately told us that he had lost sight of us. It was as if we had flown into a tunnel. Just as we were about to wave it off, we picked up the runway's centreline lights and landed. Relaying this information to our wingman, and calling out our runway positions, he was able to land behind us.

'The sandstorm was so bad that we were forced to taxi back to our line at a snail's pace, with lighting normally visible at a mile only becoming identifiable when directly abeam us. As it turns out, the "Black Knights" were the only aircraft able to land at Qatar that night. All of

The crew of 'Nite 111' prepare to fly a training mission soon after CV-63 ended its time in the NAG on 17 April 2003. The top two rows of LGBs in the bomb log on this aircraft represent the ordnance dropped by 'Nite 111' in OIF, while the bottom row (applied to the Tomcat in red) denotes a portion of the bomb log for 'Nite 104' (BuNo 158620), which crashed in Iraq on 2 April 2003. The latter jet had expended 18 LGBs by the time it was lost, and silhouettes for these were applied to 'Nites 107', '110' and '111'. Aside from this single loss, VF-154 achieved outstanding serviceability (the unit flew 286 combat sorties and recorded a 100 per cent combat sortie-completion rate) with its fleet of 12 elderly F-14As, surpassing the other Tomcat units in-theatre. This was primarily because so many A-model units had been 'put down' early on in the Tomcat phase-out, leaving a large stock of spare parts that were unique to the F-14A. With the jet on the verge of retirement, all parts were viewed as consumables by VF-154, and when something broke it was discarded, rather than repaired. This was not the case for the F-14B/D, however, which had specific avionics and computers that were shared assets, and which had to be repaired and not just replaced when they developed a fault (*PH3 Todd Frantom*)

Aviation Ordnancemen get to work loading GBU-12s to a VF-154 jet aboard CV-63 in late March 2003. The unit expended 358 LGBs between 21 March and 14 April, flying primarily FAC(A) and SCAR missions. Like VF-2, VF-154 was also involved in TF-20 SOF support sorties, although these missions were flown exclusively by the shore-based crews. The latter had the advantage of briefing with their CAS assets for these TCT missions. A VF-2 RIO who got to operate with VF-154 on two TF-20 missions recalled;

'I think that our situational awareness (SA) in the F-14D was much better when taking over from them during the operations I was involved in, but that was a direct reflection of the equipment that we had at our disposal in our upgraded Tomcats, not on the aircrew themselves. On the two TF-20 missions that I flew (a third was cancelled at the last minute), the VF-154 crews did most of the asset set up and covered the rather uneventful ingress into the objective area, while the main effort, target objective and egress were covered by VF-2 aircrew. Things were much more dynamic after the kick off, and JTIDS provided an additional level of deconfliction and SA as to where the other assets were at any given time during the mission. VF-154 did, however, fly many CAS/FAC(A) missions (not TF-20 related) without any VF-2 involvement, and performed them very well' (*PH3 Todd Frantom*)

our USAF and Coalition buddies were ordered to divert and sit by their aircraft all night, before returning the following morning.'

While the specifics relating to what was bombed, and just how the Al Udeid detachment went about servicing its numerous targets, remain largely classified, it has been revealed that these crews were responsible for developing new tactics, techniques and procedures for operating with multi-service SOF teams. The five crews flew daily missions specifically briefed to support individual ground units, and in one 48-hour period the 'Black Knights' detachment flew 14 sorties, totalling over 100 hours of flight time.

According to VF-154's post-cruise summary of its contribution to OIF, FAC(A) crews on the beach amassed more than 300 combat hours and delivered in excess of 50,000 lbs of ordnance (98 GBU-12s) in 21 days of flying with their five jets. Despite its success, this unique operation is unlikely to be repeated again according to Cdr Waters;

'Since naval aviators do not like to ask permission to use someone else's runway for combat operations, the Al Udeid detachment is not likely a model for the future. However, it did lay the foundation, in both tactics and trust, for future operations between Navy FAC(A)s and joint ground and SOF in support of National Command Authority objectives.'

JET DOWN

VF-154 did not escape from its shore-based foray unscathed, however, for on the night of 1 April NSAWC augmentees Lt Chad Vincelette and Lt Cdr Scotty 'Gordo' McDonald (RIO) were forced to eject over southern Iraq when their jet (F-14A BuNo 158620) suffered a single (port) engine and fuel transfer system failure. The latter caused the remaining engine to run dry too, so the crew, who were two hours into their mission (and having already dropped some of their LGBs), ejected.

Within minutes, a pilot in an orbiting U-2 from the USAF's 9th Reconnaissance Wing picked up a signal from the crew's survival radios and passed the information back to his mission controller at Beale Air Force Base, in California. The latter in turn contacted CENTCOM's Joint Personnel Recovery Center, which quickly despatched a USAF 301st Rescue Squadron Combat Search and Rescue HH-60G (supported by TACAIR assets) from Al Jaber air base in Kuwait. The naval aviators were rescued a short while later. This F-14A was the first Coalition aircraft to crash in Iraq since the start of OIF.

Lt Vincelette later gave the following account of what went wrong with his jet to *Stars and Stripes* magazine upon his return to CV-63;

'We were heading out of Iraq after a normal flight, looking for a tanker to refuel from, when the left engine failed. Next came a failure in the fuel transfer system that allows the good engine to use all the aircraft's fuel.

There was nothing we could do but sit and watch the fuel count down. We knew what was coming, and when it dipped below 200 lbs, the right engine came down, the generator started to hiccup and it was time to go.

'"Gordo" yelled "Eject, Eject, Eject!" while I was doing my best to keep the jet stable to ensure that we were in a good envelope so when we punched out the 'chutes would work as advertised. "Gordo" initiated the ejection. It was a fairly surreal experience, as we went from sitting in the warmth and comfort of our own cockpit to a violent windblast and hitting the desert floor pretty hard in our 'chutes. Once on the ground, I quickly met up with "Gordo" and asked him whether he could walk as I helped him onto his feet. He replied, "I can *run* – just point the way!"'

ON THE BOAT

With the majority of VF-154's senior officers ashore at Al Udeid, it was left to XO Cdr Doug Waters to ensure that the remaining seven jets and ten crews aboard CV-63 made a valuable contribution to the CAS mission assigned to CVW-5. The 'Black Knights' left on the boat were primarily junior officers, and they proved more than up to the task at hand as they manned the 'JO flying club' which expended 246 GBU-12s, ten GBU-16s and four GBU-10s during 27 days of combat. Cdr Waters detailed a typical carrier-based mission for the unit during OIF;

'We would launch as a section or division from the carrier, transiting to a tanker track and topping off either in northern Saudi Arabia or southern Iraq, before checking in with an E-3 AWACS or Navy E-2 and receiving tasking. We would then rely on the F-14's LTS to search our assigned area for tanks, artillery, troop emplacements etc. When we

Having selected full military power, which has ignited the afterburners, the crew of 'Nite 105' (BuNo 161271) prepare for a night launch from CV-63 in early April 2003. Operating as the dedicated CAS air wing, CVW-5 performed an equal number of day and night sorties in OIF. This particular F-14 dropped 24 LGBs during the campaign. Delivered to the Navy in May 1981, the aircraft initially served with VF-124, before being assigned to VF-111 in 1982. BuNo 161271 was transferred to VF-2 in 1986, and duly saw combat in *Desert Storm* with the unit from the flightdeck of USS *Ranger* (CV-61) in 1991. The aircraft joined VF-211 following VF-2's transition onto the F-14D in 1993, and it remained with the 'Fighting Checkmates' until flown to Japan on 4 July 2001 to join VF-154. The jet returned to Oceana with the unit in September 2003 (*PH3 T Frantom*)

Laden down with four GBU-12s, 'Nite 103' takes flight after being shot off one of CV-63's waist catapults to signal the start of yet another OIF mission. The jet would return to the carrier three hours later (*PH3 Todd Frantom*)

located the enemy, we would engage them with our standard load of four GBU-12s, and if there were enough targets, we would call in other airborne fighters and provide them with precise coordinates in order to let them finish off the job. We would also buddy-lase for other aircraft such as CVW-5's F/A-18s so as to ensure the quick and efficient destruction of smaller, hard to find targets that our LTS pods were able to see but other platforms had difficulty acquiring.

A pilot checks the guidance vanes on a GBU-24 Paveway III LGB. The weapon's larger stabilisation package on the back allows it travel farther in flight (*PH3 Todd Frantom*)
Below
The pilot of 'Nite 107' (BuNo 161296) has activated the port wing spoilers so as to level his heavy jet off after the cat shot (*PH3 Todd Frantom*)

Bottom
VF-154 post-OIF in May 2003

'Normally, having serviced a target, we would head south to the tanker to replenish our tanks, before pressing back into Iraq in order to have one more go round in the same – or different – kill box, before hitting the tanker again on our way back to the ship. Our missions lasted between three and three-and-a-half hours.'

The shore detachment returned to CV-63 in the second week of April, and by the end of the aerial campaign on the 14th of that month, VF-154 had dropped no fewer than 358 LGBs, buddy-lased 65 more and passed target coordinates for 32 JDAM during the course of 286 sorties. These totals meant that the 'Black Knights' had expended more ordnance than any other unit in CVW-5, despite flying the oldest jets in the air wing.

NORTHERN WAR

The OIF war waged by Mediterranean-based air wings CVW-3 and CVW-8, embarked in the carriers *Harry S Truman* and *Theodore Roosevelt* respectively, contrasted markedly with that fought by their NAG-based brethren, as CVW-3's Public Affairs Officer Lt(jg) Jason Rojas explained in the air wing's cruise summary;

'With Turkey denying the US Army's 4th Infantry Division use of its territory as a jumping-off point, northern-front activities centred around SOF activity, with some teams as small as three individuals. The teams relied heavily on CAS from CVW-3 and CVW-8, aircraft from both air wings often putting ordnance dangerously close to friendly forces. The support these aircraft provided undoubtedly saved the lives of Coalition forces on the ground, and eventually led to the capitulation of nearly 100,000 Iraqi soldiers.'

Prior to dedicating themselves to flying SOF CAS sorties, CVW-3's VF-32 and CVW-8's VF-213 had undertaken conventional strike missions with JDAM and LGBs against fixed targets in Iraq. These sorties, flown at the start of the conflict, were some of the longest of the war, covering distances of up to 1400 miles one way. As the Tomcat had proven in OEF, it was more than capable of handling such sorties, and the mission lead for these strikes was often an F-14 crew. Indeed, the first CVW-3 mission of the war was led by *Desert Storm* veteran, and VF-32 CO, Cdr Marcus Hitchcock, with his CAG, Capt Mark Vance, as his RIO. Hitchcock explained the complex routing problems that his air wing, and CVW-8, faced in the first 72 hours of OIF;

'In the lead up to our first mission, the political situation in the area was a little topsy-turvy to say the least. We didn't know whether we would be heading in via Turkey or not. This meant that we had to plan a series of different routes into Iraq – northerly, central and southerly. This uncertainty prevailed until the diplomats figured out which way we could go. Launching from just off the Nile Delta, we were allowed to proceed down the Sinai Peninsula, around the southern tips of Israel and Jordan, across the Saudi Arabian desert and then finally into Iraq.

'Approval for this route was given just 24 hours before the start of OIF, and a lot of the supporting tanker assets were not given the word that they needed to be in a certain location in order to facilitate our first strikes.

'Nineteen aircraft launched on the first mission on 22 March, and we ended up with 13 pressing south to Iraq. The remaining aircraft – four S-3s and two E-2s – did some up front tanking and command and control, before turning back to the ship at a pre-briefed point, leaving the strike aircraft to push into Iraq. It was a very long transit – 1400 miles one way – to the target, although we endured this part of the mission a little more comfortably in our Tomcats than our strike brethren did in their Hornets. We got to the Saudi Arabia-Iraq border and rendezvoused with out first "big wing" tankers. The subsequent refuelling session was interesting to say the least, because tankers were showing up at the

Opposite right
Cdr Marcus Hitchcock (seated), CVW-3 CO Capt Mark Vance (behind Hitchcock) and an unidentified pilot from VF-32 watch LTS weapon impact footage imagery on a portable Sony Hi-8 player in CVN-75's CVIC immediately after returning from *Truman's* first OIF strike. CVIC is the first stop that the aircrew make post-flight to ensure that accurate and timely BHA reports are generated by the air wing and sent to the CAOC. Using the same format as the mission recorders fitted into Navy TACAIR jets, Hi-8 is a crucial tool in the BHA process, as it allows tapes to be swiftly reviewed at debrief stations aboard ship. This means that multiple debriefs can be conducted at once, rather than crews having to wait their turn to access the players permanently built into CVIC. Maintainers also use the portable Hi-8 system to troubleshoot mission recorders on the flightdeck.
As the mission lead, Cdr Hitchcock had given the pre-flight briefing for the strike, and of this event he recalled;
'We had a full air wing huddle for the first mission. The striking thing for me was the sheer number of press that attended the brief – they almost outnumbered the participating aircrew! We specifically constructed two briefs to cater for the embedded media coverage. The first one went into as much detail as I could in an open forum, and that took about 15 minutes to present. I covered things like the general routing that we would follow, the targets we were going after, weather conditions and the number of jets heading into Iraq. We then stopped, the media left, and I started the brief over again. This time I went into the various aspects of the mission in much greater detail'
(PH1 Michael Pendergrass)

designated rendezvous point just as we were having to make the decision as to whether to divert aircraft through a lack of fuel.

'We got to the USAF tankers just in time, but not before losing two Hornets that were timed out before they could refuel – we had a set vul time that we had to be in Iraq for, and once that was up we had to leave enemy air space so as not to conflict with follow-up strikes. The tankers were late arriving on station, and it took so long to refuel us that the last two Hornets could not be topped off in time to allow us all to get in and out in our briefed vul slot. I therefore headed into Iraq with only 11 jets.

'Pre-OIF, we had trained with our Tomcats loaded up with three JDAM. No other unit had sortied with more than two weapons up to that point, as the jet was very heavy on the controls at cruising altitude when fuelled for combat, carrying defensive missiles and three 2000-lb bombs. We trained hard in this configuration once in the Mediterranean, and this training paid off in OIF.

'Hitting our targets at Al Taqaddum air base on that first night, my crews did spectacular work with their JDAM. We knew about the weapon's capability in theory, but it was not until we had each delivered our three bombs smack onto our targets, spread across the airfield, within a matter of seconds that it became readily apparent that this was a new kind of weapon, the likes of which we had never seen before.

'We were opposed by localised AAA as we approached the target, but we easily avoided this at our run-in height of between 28,000 ft and 33,000 ft. As we came across an airfield on our departure from the target, we saw three SA-2 SAMs launch. We had already dropped our JDAM by then, and these did not need targeting support, so we were able to go to 100 per cent power and defeat the SAMs through tactical manoeuvring.'

VF-32 RIO Lt Cdr Dave Dorn was involved in the follow-up daylight strike that launched before the first wave had returned to the carrier, the unit despatching a division of three F-14Bs. He too was impressed with JDAM, which he was employing for the first time;

'The JDAM is a force multiplier above the LTS because the latter system only allows us to guide one weapon at a time. Three JDAM-equipped jets can do the same amount of work as nine Tomcats carrying LGBs. We had 11 jets go over the target, all of which were

Below
Carrying a mixed load of GBU-12s and JDAM, three F-14Bs from VF-32 prepare to be directed out to the catapults in OIF. Like all other Tomcat units assigned to the war, VF-32 chose to remove the door which covered the refuelling probes on their aircraft. This modification was done in an effort to prevent the probe being damaged when refuelling from a USAF KC-135, which has been dubbed the 'Iron Maiden' by Navy TACAIR crews over the years due to the unforgiving nature of the basket fitted to the Stratotanker. The latter has inflicted much damage to the F-14 because of its short hose and heavy basket, which could rip the probe door off and send it down the starboard intake into the engine. This in turn could result in the loss of the starboard engine at minimum or, at worst, a fire (*US NAVY*)

so we took a day off and repositioned the carrier further northeast in the Mediterranean. Once CVW-3 started the second phase of its campaign by launching attacks on northern Iraq, we found ourselves consistently flying 12 sorties per day for the rest of the war.

'We were pleased with the way the jets and the crews had performed in the first two missions of OIF, but we were now unsure of how to fight the war once we got word that we were heading north to start flying through Turkey. The missions flown on the 22nd had been pre-planned fixed strikes. Each crew knew exactly what it was going to attack well before it launched, having trained up to hit these targets for several weeks in advance. As we headed for Turkey, our mission changed, and we were no longer sure of what we were going to attack. From then on, when we strapped into our jets on the flightdeck we rarely knew where the target was and what would be defending it.

'For the first few days in the north, we were scratching around for some fixed targets to hit so that we could at least conduct some rudimentary pre-mission planning, thus allowing us to familiarise ourselves with the procedural aspects of working in this theatre. Things did not turn out this way, however. We would brief to attack a certain target, but by the time we had launched, the situation on the ground had invariably changed. Effectively, this meant that the only pre-flight planning that we could perform on the ship centred on where the tanker support was located, what frequency it would be using and what weather we could expect over the target. If it was cloudy we would take JDAM, and if it was clear we would use LGBs, as they were more mission flexible. We also flew with a mix of both on occasions in order to hedge our bets!

'We conducted limited-brief missions over northern Iraq with SOF teams on the ground from 24 March to 18 April. Unlike in the south, where there was a clear line between the good guys and the bad guys, in the north, we never had a clearly developed battlefield that boasted a discernable frontline. We therefore tailored our operations towards servicing one or more of the 40 to 50 kill boxes that we had divided northern Iraq up into. Crews rarely knew which one they would be assigned to prior to launching from the ship. We would be allocated a kill box to service en route to Iraq, the decision on where we would be heading being made by our AWACS controllers after they had checked "on trade" with SOF guys on the ground.

'Occasionally, we would break out of the kill box mentality and hit targets within a small geographic region that was perhaps being worked over as part of a ground offensive by peshmerga militiamen, or we would alternate between targets in several areas during the course of one sortie.

'The Iraqis had three corps of ground troops in the north. Our mission was to keep these soldiers occupied so that they could not head south to help defend Baghdad from V Corps and the 1st MEF. This task was given to two air wings, controlling 72 Hornets and 20

Both VF-32 and VF-213 regularly carried mixed weapon loads in OIF, this 'Blacklions' jet boasting a GBU-12 and a GBU-31(V)2/B. VF-213 pilot Lt Cdr Marc Hudson explained the thinking behind such a load-out;

'With the Tomcat capable of employing both JDAM and LGBs, we could service two different targets during the course of one CAS mission – we often sortied with a mixed load towards the end of the war. Such a mix proved to be lethal to the enemy, because we had instances where the ground FAC was giving us GPS coordinates for the JDAM and we were able to lock the target up with our LTS pod. We then chose to go with the laser precision weapon instead. Should the target not have been destroyed first time round, we could make a correction with the JDAM off the laser-guided drop and come back and hit it again with clinical precision. Such a weapons mix really allowed us to cover virtually all the targets encountered on a daily basis in OIF. A penetration target would have been the only thing that we would have had to weaponeer for, conducting deep pre-mission planning accordingly' (VF-213)

Tomcats, and 1000 SOF guys on the ground, supported by Kurdish freedom fighters. The SOF squads operated throughout northern Iraq, and they were responsible for finding us targets.

'In general, we would launch from the carrier and head to the border between Turkey and Iraq, where we would tank for the first time – we were at half gas when we meet the tanker inbound to the target area. We would then head into Iraq for about 45 minutes and work the targets. If we expended all of our weapons we would fly straight home. If not, we would find the tanker once again and then head back into Iraq for another 45 minutes, before returning home, again via the tanker. We would effectively cover a two-hour block on a typical sortie, whether we deployed our weapons or not, and then be replaced on station by a second wave from the ship. Each wave usually consisted of a section of two F-14s and up to four sections of F/A-18s. These jets were supported by a single EA-6B, with an E-2 providing AWACS control and several S-3s airborne over the carrier with tactical gas should we need it upon our return.'

One of the first missions undertaken by VF-213 upon CVN-71's arrival off Turkey was to provide DCA and CAS support for the airborne assault on Irbil air base by 1000 paratroopers of the US Army's 173rd Airborne Brigade on 26 March. Conducting the largest parachute drop since World War 2, the soldiers jumped from 15 USAF C-17 Globemaster IIs that were escorted by three waves of strike aircraft from CVW-8. One of those involved was VF-213 pilot Lt Cdr Larry Sidbury;

'I shot FLIR video of the paratroopers as they jumped out of the back of the C-17s that night. It was sobering to think that these guys would be relying exclusively on us to aid their efforts on the ground as they pushed out to attack targets around Tikrit, Kirkuk and Mosul. We had ordnance on our jets ready to support the landings should they be resisted either from the air or the ground, but there were no enemy forces to be seen. We eventually left the area once the transports had headed back into Turkey and dropped our bombs on pre-planned targets around Kirkuk.'

WEATHER ISSUES

Operations over northern Iraq were blighted by poor weather for much of OIF, and seasoned naval aviators with more than 15 years of fast jet flying experience told the Author that they had never encountered such conditions before. One of those grappling with solid cloud and extreme turbulence on a near daily basis was VF-213's XO, Cdr John Hefti;

'We routinely tanked in the clouds, being buffeted by thunderstorms and turbulence in weather fronts that stretched from ground level up to 40,000 ft. Once in Iraq, the bad weather made it difficult for us to acquire targets with our FLIR. As it transpired, flying to and from the targets at night in these conditions posed a greater danger to us than the Iraqis.

'Although I had seen combat in the Tomcat in both *Desert Storm* and OEF, those night missions in OIF were some of the most challenging flights I have ever had to perform as a naval aviator. I had experienced bad weather in *Desert Storm* on only two or three occasions, when we had to tank in clouds, and in Afghanistan the skies were generally clear. In OIF, by contrast, at least half of our sorties were flown in poor to bad weather, where we stayed IFR virtually from the minute we got over Turkey until we came back out of the Mediterranean and headed for the boat four or

This amazing photograph of a GBU-12 heading for its target was taken by a TARPS-equipped VF-32 jet. The aircraft's RIO was Lt Cdr David Dorn, who recalled;

'We were flying the TARPS jet when we were fragged to hit an SA-2 site with an LGB. Skipper Hitchcock was flying the jet which lased the target for our weapon. We got some great TARPS footage of the LGB coming off of our jet and heading down to impact the missile site. I got to replicate this mission several days later, when we again hit a target with an LGB while flying the TARPS jet. The jet could only carry LGBs when equipped with the TARPS as the JDAM was just too big. And when carrying the TARPS pod we could not employ the LTS, so we had to rely on our wingman to buddy lase for us.'

VF-32 flew very few TARPS missions in OIF, as squadron CO Cdr Marcus Hitchcock explained;

'Although we were not tasked with flying TARPS missions in the early stages of the campaign, I made sure that our dedicated reconnaissance crews flew a couple of sorties in order to remain current with the system, and to allow VF-32 to offer this service to CVW-3 should it be required. We were eventually tasked to fly several missions later in the war. My squadron operated both conventional and CD TARPS, and they effectively complemented each other. Because we were so pressed with servicing ground targets, we decided to load the TARPS jets with bombs too so that they could fly a dual mission' (*VF-32*) five hours later. Thankfully, for some reason the weather never actually seemed to reach the carrier. We were still faced with a night trap though, which is always far more difficult than a daylight recovery.'

Despite the constant threat posed by the weather, both VF-32 and VF-213 did their best to maintain 24-hour TACAIR support for the SOF teams in Iraq. Lt Cdr Larry Sidbury was one of those pilots who worked closely with SOF FACs in the north at night. Here, he explains how a routine OIF CAS sortie in the north was performed;

'Typically, we would launch from the boat and head southeast over Turkey, hitting the tanker over the border with Iraq. With our tanks topped off, we would call up our AWACS controller and tell him we were ready for mission tasking. We would let him know what type of aircraft we were flying, what ordnance we were carrying, our fuel state and whether we were FAC(A) qualified or not. We would then be given a tasking, which usually consisted of location coordinates and a frequency for our ground FAC, or the coordinates for a kill box.

'Heading into northern Iraq as a section of two jets, or occasionally as a division of four, the strike lead would head towards the ground FAC's location and then attempt to raise him on the radio. In most cases, the SOF FACs were using hand-held radios, and you almost needed to be overhead their position to talk to them, particularly when they were working in the mountains east of Mosul and Kirkuk. They usually had tasking for you right away, so they were ready to accept your ordnance as soon as you checked in. The 9-line brief that the FAC would give you would be short, clipped and concise – these guys were big on comms brevity, and you certainly got the impression that they did not want to talk on the radio for any extended period of time.

'A 9-line attack brief is the key element in effective CAS, as it should have all of the information needed to ingress, conduct the attack and egress the target area. The components of the brief are as follows;

1) Initial Point (IP) – location from where CAS jet begins attack run
2) Bearing/offset – bearing IP to target, offset direction (left/right)
3) Distance – distance to target from IP in nautical miles for jets
4) Elevation – elevation of target in feet/metres above Mean Sea Level
5) Target Description
6) Target Location – coordinates for target
7) Mark – type of visual or Laser/IR mark that FAC puts on/near target
8) Friendlies – bearing and distance from target to nearest friendly unit. (not coordinates so as to minimise confusion with target coordinates)
9) Egress – direction and IP for the CAS aircraft to fly after attacking the target in order to clear the area

'Additional information is provided after the 9-line brief to include Time-on-Target (time when CAS aircraft's bombs must hit the target) and Final Attack Heading/Cone (either a heading or an arc of headings that the CAS jet must fly down when delivering weapons onto the target).

'This information would be relayed to you via radio, and we literally had a phonebook of frequencies on which the FACs would be operating, as there were hundreds of small three-man teams servicing targets across northern Iraq. Each team had at least two radios, and these all needed to have unique frequencies. Nine times out of ten, the frequency you would end up working on wouldn't be in the book! One of the nice things about

LGB-toting 'Blacklion 107' (BuNo 161166) is marshalled into position over waist catapult three on 1 April 2003 (*PH3 Matthew Bash*)

His all-important radio secured in his webbing, a SOF ground FAC goes in search of his next target (*USMC*)

flying the F-14 was that you had a RIO, and he/she could run the radios while you concentrated on flying the jet. This proved vital in OIF when dealing with both AWACS controllers and ground FACs.

'The latter would not talk to the AWACS controller at all, dealing instead through another agency with more powerful communications equipment, which would in turn contact the AWACS to inform them that they had tasking in-theatre. We would be passed this information, along with the FAC's frequency, and we would talk directly with the ground controller. Both the RIO and I would write down the FAC's 9-line brief onto our kneeboards. We then read back the coordinates to him to check that we had copied them correctly, and he would confirm with a simple "Yes", or a mike click. We then punched the coordinates into the bomb guidance system, after which I verified with my RIO that I was working with the same target information as he/she was.

'With all the targeting parameters confirmed, we then started working up a game plan on how best to attack the target. A lot of the time, we worked the target in a textbook way, having briefed for just this type of mission back on the ship. We would tailor our general tactics to suit the situation at hand, confident in the knowledge that we had our training to fall back on should the target prove difficult to hit.

'With the jet set up correctly and the target locked up by the LTS, the bomb symbology in the HUD would tell us exactly when to release either the JDAM or the LGB. With all the release parameters met, I would tell the FAC that we were set up for our run in to the target, giving him the "wings level" call, which would prompt his reply of "Cleared Hot". I now had his authority to release ordnance – I could not do so without his say so.

'Once the FAC had declared our targets "hostile", I was happy to drop my bombs. His view of the enemy was far better than mine, so the final call on whether to release ordnance or not was ultimately his to make. I never questioned his decision at all.

Flying over snow-covered mountains on the Turkey-Iraq border on 10 April 2003, 'Blacklion 105' (BuNo 161163) tops off its tanks from a Akrotiri-based 100th ARW KC-135R. Such clear conditions were exceptional in OIF, as Lt Cdr Larry Sidbury explained;

'Tanking was a miserable experience pretty well throughout OIF, as you would invariably have to join on a tanker which was socked in the clouds. Some nights you would get to within a mile of the tanker before you could break out its lights and control your closure. You had to get your approach right the first time in such poor weather, as disorientation could have easily proven fatal in the solid cloud we often had to rendezvous in' (*VF-213*)

Having completed its refuelling, VF-32's CAG jet (BuNo 162916) drops away from a 163rd ARW KC-135R on 11 April 2003. This aircraft dropped 30 LGBs and five JDAM during 35 OIF missions (*Paul Farley*)

'I often dealt with FACs who were under fire. In those cases, you might see enemy vehicles on the ground, and you would be fully aware of his situation. I would be in constant communication with him, telling him what I could see, and he would use this information to confirm my targets. I would be cleared by the FAC to engage those targets, after which I required no further information from him in order to do my job. Usually, when you hit vehicles or troops on the move that were in close contact with a SOF team, things settled down for a awhile as the enemy took cover. This allowed the FAC to tell you where the "next alligator closest to the canoe" was, and you could start working the new target.

'Things could rapidly get dynamic in these close contact situations, and you had to be very sure that you were targeting bad guys and not friendlies before you dropped your bombs. I would remain in continual contact with the FAC during such engagements, constantly questioning him on the radio as to the orientation and direction of the vehicles that we could see, or where his placement was in relation to a nearby river or road.

'One night we helped a FAC out who had positioned himself on a small hill in order to improve his view of a main road that ran between Mosul and Kirkuk. Somehow, his position was compromised to the extent that a convoy of Iraqi Army vehicles detoured off the road that he had under observation and surrounded him. They jumped out of their trucks and started engaging him with small arms and mortar fire. The FAC was screaming on the radio for assistance, and he gave us a hasty plot of his location. As it turned out, we found it easy to target the enemy troops thanks to the way their vehicles ended up oriented around the FAC. He was able to give us a very quick visual talk-on, and we soon had bombs on the enemy positions that allowed the FAC to make good his escape.

'On a typical CAS mission, a two-ship F-14 section would operate with one to two miles' separation between jets, with my wingman keeping a visual lock on us at all times, and vice versa. Such separation ensured that you had room to manoeuvre without the fear of running into each other. Despite always operating as a section, we usually worked separate targets, although we would both be flying in the same general area.

'We would also be employing the services of the same FAC, who normally had multiple targets in the same area. They might be a mile or so apart, or sometimes they were closer to each other than that. The FAC would have a list of targets that needed servicing, and looking out on the battlefield from his position, they would all be in the same general area from his perspective.

'My wingman and I were sent to work with a FAC near Kirkuk towards the end of the war. On our last run in on the target, three SAMs came up in front of my section, launched with plenty of lead. We started to defend against these missiles, and there was some excitement on the radio between the two jets as we performed some tight manoeu-

A section of VF-32 jets take up station off the left wing of a KC-135 prior to taking on fuel at the mid-way point in their mission over Iraq. Both jets appear to have expended a single LGB apiece, as only a solitary GBU-12 can be seen beneath each F-14B. The Tomcat nearest to the camera is BuNo 163224, which flew 35 sorties in OIF and dropped 29 LGBs and 14 JDAM. The second jet is BuNo 161608, which dropped 28 LGBs and 14 JDAM during the course of 42 sorties. VF-32 was involved in the worst friendly fire incident of OIF when, on 6 April 2003, one of its crews was cleared by a SOF ground FAC to attack an Iraqi tank that had targeted a convoy of Kurdish special forces near Dibakan, 30 miles southeast of Mosul. A single LGB was dropped, and this struck the 18-vehicle SOF/Kurdish convoy, rather than the tank. Some 18 Kurdish fighters, four US soldiers and a BBC translator were killed, with a further 80 people injured. A post-war investigation into the incident found that the pilot had been erroneously cleared to drop his LGB without the benefit of target coordinates from the FAC, as the latter was 'operating under great stress' at the time. The F-14 crew had spotted a knocked out tank alongside the intersection where the Coalition convoy had stopped, and they had mistakenly identified this as their target. The pilot radioed the FAC and told him 'I see a road, I see an intersection, I see vehicles', to which the FAC replied, with tragic consequences, 'Roger, that's your target, you're cleared to fire' (*USAF*)

vres to defeat the apparently ballistic SAMs. I was trying to talk the other crew's eyes onto the missiles, and although they never saw them, they reacted positively to our calls and broke off in the right direction. We then came over the top of their aeroplane in an effort to reorient our section and continue our flow to the north. I was in afterburner at the time, and the junior RIO in the second jet shouted over the radio that he could see the missiles right above his cockpit! The pilot looked up in response to the call and quickly informed his RIO that his "missiles" were their strike lead! The RIO caught a lot of heat about that call for the rest of the cruise.'

By the time VF-32 and VF-213 ceased combat operations in OIF on 19 April, the 20 Tomcats flying from the two carriers in the eastern Mediterranean had dropped an astounding 652,600 lbs of ordnance in just 30 days. VF-32's 14 crews had flown 275 combat sorties totalling 1247 flight hours, with a 100 per cent sortie completion rate. The unit had expended 247 LGBs and 118 JDAM, as well as firing 1128 rounds of 20 mm high explosive incendiary in strafing passes. VF-213's aircrew, having summed up their OIF experiences with the phrase 'living after midnight, bombing 'til dawn' following their myriad nocturnal 'Vampire' missions, had completed 198 sorties totalling 907 flight hours. Also achieving a 100 per cent sortie completion rate, VF-213 had delivered 102 LGBs and 94 JDAM during the course of the campaign.

Coalition troops on the ground greatly appreciated the effort put in by CVW-3 and CVW-8 on their behalf, in spite of the often inclement weather. Their feelings were accurately summed up Col Charles Cleveland, Commander Joint Special Operations Task Force-North, in the following e-mail message sent to CVW-3's CAG, Capt Mark Vance, just days after major hostilities had ended in late April 2003;

'On behalf of Special Force A teams and the rest of us here at TF *Viking*, I want to say thanks for being there when we needed you. You were instrumental in our dismantling three IZ Corps and the ultimate capture of the third and fourth largest cities in Iraq. Says a lot considering the Coalition ground component largely consisted of the 10th Special Force Group (Airborne) and our Kurdish allies. We took big risks knowing that when we needed you, you'd be there. You never failed us, and as a direct result we never lost a position and had only four casualties during the entire operation.'

'Gypsy 112' races over the Mediterranean at high speed, having delivered all of its ordnance. CVW-3 worked VF-32's crews, and their jets, hard in OIF, as Cdr Hitchcock recalled;

'With only 14 crews in the squadron, and an intensive mission requirement from the very start of OIF, we relied heavily on the junior pilots and RIOs to take on the responsibility of section leaders. We had worked hard to ensure that we had trained up sufficient individuals to act as section leaders prior to the war starting. This paid dividends, as it allowed VF-32 to sortie 12 jets per day. We even tried to launch 14 on one day, managing 13 instead. In the end, 12 sorties a day was all we could realistically manage due the fact we had just 14 crews in the squadron. We were not limited by the availability of jets, but aircrew. Our missions turned out to be so long in duration that a single crew could only fly one sortie per day.

'CVW-3 would cover one half of the day, and CVW-8 the other half, and in the 12 hours that we were the active carrier, I would use everyone. The two crews that did not fly would be manning the LSO, squadron and air wing watches that the unit had to stand as was typical for a squadron at sea. This meant that every squadron member was fully employed every single day in OIF. When I tried for the 14-mission push, we found that were scratching around trying to find people to stand watches' (*VF-32*)

ONGOING OPERATIONS

On 1 May 2003, President George W Bush stood on the flightdeck of CVN-72 and declared that major hostilities in Iraq were over. By then, the only carrier in the region was *Nimitz*, on station in the NAG. As previously mentioned, the vessel was bereft of Tomcats, as its embarked air wing – CVW-11 – had made history by becoming the first to venture into the NAG without an F-14 component. Indeed, it was not until 23 October 2003 that the unmistakeable shape of the Tomcat was seen in the skies over Iraq once again following the arrival of VF-211 in-theatre aboard CVN-65.

Assigned to CVW-1, this unit was also making history, as it was conducting the very last operational cruise of the F-14A. Unable to employ JDAM, which had again become the weapon of choice post-OIF, VF-211 saw very little action during its time in the NAG, or during its brief spell in support of OEF. As with all Tomcat units that have ventured into the NAG since May 2003, VF-211 spent most of its time flying TARPS missions or performing show of force and ground convoy patrols over Main/Alternate Supply Routes. Very occasionally, the unit also got to provide LTS assistance to the three Hornet squadrons assigned to CVW-1, which dropped a handful of JDAM using target coordinates provided by the Tomcat.

VF-211's 'Nickel 102' (BuNo 162610) is launched from one of CVN-65's waist catapults on 18 November 2003. Seconds later, the F/A-18A+ of VMFA-312 seen on bow catapult two would also be launched, and the two jets would form up for a mixed section ISR (Intelligence, Surveillance and Reconnaissance) patrol of southern Iraq. Delivered new to VF-1 in early 1987, BuNo 162610 was passed on to VF-51 in 1989. The aircraft joined VF-213 following the 'Screaming Eagles'' disestablishment on 31 March 1995. The jet completed a single *WestPac* with the 'Blacklions', after which it was one of six jets that the unit sent to Japan to serve with VF-154 in March 1997. Returning to Oceana in July 2001 and joining VF-211, the jet was finally stricken when the unit retired its last Tomcats in September 2004 (*PH Milosz Reterski*)

By the end of the deployment in February 2004, VF-211 had flown 220 combat sorties. Despite the unit not dropping any ordnance, its CO, Cdr Mike Whetstone, was proud of the squadron's performance;

'Most of our accolades have come due to our TARPS missions for the strike group commander and the task force commander on the ground. Each day we'd send two or three aircraft over Iraq or Afghanistan, while the rest conducted training missions. Our F-14s were the oldest in the Navy's inventory, so it took a lot to get them into the air. But the maintainers treated them like they would a classic car. It was a real challenge for them, but they handled it like pros.'

Replacing CVN-65 on station in the NAG was USS *George Washington* (CVN-73), with CVW-7 embarked. The latter boasted two F-14B units within its ranks, VF-11 and VF-143 making their last deployments with the jet prior to transitioning to Super Hornets. Unlike VF-211, both squadrons would get to deliver ordnance in combat during their time in the NAG following a dramatic increase in insurgent activity across the country. The first bomb drops by F-14s took place on 28/29 April, as CVW-7 was called on to provide direct fire support for the 1st MEF, which had 'troops in contact' with enemy forces in Falluja – a stronghold of the insurgency. Some 17 GBU-12 LGBs were dropped by F-14s and F/A-18s during the 40 sorties flown in this 48-hour period.

With CVW-7 fielding near equal numbers of Tomcats (20) and Hornets (24), the two types operated very closely with each other over Iraq, as VF-11 CO Cdr Scott Moyer explained;

'In order to enhance our mission capabilities, we decided to fly mixed sections over Iraq. We also mixed our weapon load-out too, with the

Armed with two GBU-12s, VF-11's 'Ripper 201' (BuNo 162912) comes under tension on CVN-73's bow catapult one in the NAG in June 2004. Only the third F-14B built, this aircraft was delivered to VF-24 in February 1988. It subsequently served with VF-101, VF-142, VF-143 and VF-102, prior to joining VF-11 in late 1997 when the latter unit swapped its F-14Ds for B-model Tomcats. BuNo 162912 has served as the 'Red Rippers'' CO jet since 1999, and it is due to be retired in the spring of 2005 when VF-11 completes its transition to the F/A-18F (*Erik Sleutelberg*)

Since OIF I, most Tomcats have returned from ISR patrols with their bombs still aboard. 'Ripper 210' (BuNo 162911), seen in the final stages of its recovery in June 2004, was no exception (*Erik Sleutelberg*)

Again with its LGBs still firmly attached to their shackles, VF-143's 'Dog 102' (BuNo 162921) hits the deck of CVN-73 and smokes the tyres as it snags an arrestor wire to signal the end of another ISR patrol over Iraq. Delivered new to VF-103 in the autumn of 1988, this aircraft served as the unit's CVW-17 CAG jet during *Desert Storm*. It remained with VF-103 in this capacity until the squadron assumed the identity of VF-84 in late 1995, after which it was transferred to VF-143. BuNo 162921 has remained with the 'Pukin' Dogs' ever since, even serving as 'Dog 100' for a brief spell in 1999-2000. It too is scheduled for retirement to the Aerospace Maintenance and Regeneration Center (AMARC) at Davis Monthan Air Force Base in Arizona in the spring of 2005 when VF-143 completes its F/A-18E conversion (*Erik Sleutelberg*)

Hornet carrying two 1000-lb JDAM and the Tomcat two or four LGBs. More often than not, we returned to CVN-73 with our bombs still aboard due to the fact that we were called on to fly less traditional missions over Iraq. Instead of dropping bombs, we would fly "show of force" sorties for troops that had either come under attack or were faced with a gathering mob situation. We would be asked by the ground JTAC (Joint Tactical Air Controller) to fly low passes in afterburner so as to make plenty of noise. This usually got the crowd running for cover.

'Even on the odd occasion when we were cleared to deliver bombs, these missions could also prove to be untraditional too. More than once my crews were instructed by the JTAC to drop LGBs or JDAM a short distance away from insurgent positions in urban areas so as to minimise collateral damage, but still register a presence with nearby enemy forces.'

VF-103 INTO THE ACTION

On 10 July 2004 USS *John F Kennedy* (CV-67), with CVW-17 embarked, arrived on station in the NAG to relieve CVN-73. As with the three previous Tomcat units to serve in-theatre, the air wing's VF-103 was conducting its last deployment with the F-14. Just ten days after flying its first mission over Iraq, the squadron dropped a single GBU-12 on an insurgent position near Baghdad. This set the tone for VF-103's four months in the NAG, with the unit seeing far more action than any other Tomcat squadron since the end of major hostilities in May 2003.

Mirroring previous air wing operations in the region post-OIF I, CVW-17 routinely paired up Hornets and Tomcats over Iraq. This was primarily because two of the three F/A-18C units (VFA-34 and VFA-83) aboard CV-67 were equipped with the first production examples of the Navy's newest targeting pod, the Raytheon ASQ-228 Advanced Targeting Forward-Looking Infra-Red (ATFLIR). For almost a decade the LTS has been viewed as the Navy's premier targeting pod, but according to VFA-83's Lt Cdr Matt Pothier, who used the ASQ-228 in action over Falluja, 'the ATFLIR makes the LTS look cheap'! He described the types of missions CVW-17 was flying to the Author;

'We would patrol predefined positions, tanking three to four times during a five- to seven-hour mission. We usually patrolled hot spots and protected high interest targets such as Coalition convoys, talking to our ground-based JTACs if they were embedded in the area where we were working. VFA-81, operating the older non-ATFLIR Lot X F/A-18Cs, always flew in a mixed section with VF-103, as it relied on the Tomcat's LTS pod to provide primary targeting for its LGBs.'

Falluja continued to prove a hot bed of unrest throughout CVW-17's time on station, and on 8 October 2004 the air wing helped provide aerial support over the city for Operation *Phantom Fury/Al-Fajr*. Some 10,000 Marines from the 1st MEF, supported by 5000 Iraqi Army soldiers, were tasked with flushing out an estimated 3000 insurgents in a bitter house-to-house campaign. One of the naval aviators involved in this operation was VF-103's Lt(jg) Matt Koop;

'When *Phantom Fury* kicked off, CENTCOM was concerned that large numbers of foreign fighters would come streaming over the borders from Syria and Iran to aid the insurgency in Falluja. Coalition forces had set up outposts along these borders to prevent this from happening, and an increase in the number of skirmishes in nearby towns was anticipated. Therefore, sections of fighters were pre-positioned to provide close air support to our troops in these areas if needed. And it was on one of these missions that I saw my first real action of the deployment.

'Ironically, when my pilot and I were told that we would be conducting a Syrian border patrol, we were more than a little disappointed not to be working with the Marines in Falluja, since that was where all the action seemed to be taking place.

'Our Tomcat was the lead aircraft that afternoon, flying in a mixed section with a Hornet wingman from VFA-81. I checked in with the DASC controller to tell him what our mission was, and where we had been told to patrol – we were hoping that he would give us a last-minute tasking to Falluja, but that was not to be the case. We continued westward and contacted the JTAC that we had been assigned to work with. He described the area that we would be patrolling, and pointed out a few outposts that had intermittently received fire in the previous 48 hours.

'Once we were on-station, the troops on the ground duly requested a show of force over their positions to either ward off or stir up any insurgent activity that might be brewing nearby. We bumped up the speed and dropped down to overfly their outposts low, fast and loud. Once we had completed our pass, we climbed back up and waited for their next request. Everything was still quiet, and after a while it was time to go hit the tanker and top off the tanks.

'When we checked back in, we were disappointed to hear that we had just missed some action. Apparently, two mortar rounds had been launched from a nearby field, and a pair of Marine helicopters had been launched to find the culprits. We could see a Cobra and a Huey conducting their search below us, but we were flying too fast and too high to offer much assistance. It was at this time that the JTAC told us, "Sorry boys. It just doesn't look like we have much for you fixed-wing guys to do". He told us that if we had any alternate missions, we were cleared to proceed. We didn't have any other assignments, so we told him we'd stick around in case anything else popped up.

'Literally minutes later the JTAC received a report that some of our troops patrolling a nearby town had been attacked by terrorists in a blue van. Having exchanged shots, the insurgents had sped away in their vehicle. The Marines called for immediate air support, and both our

VF-103's Lt(jg) Matt Koop sits on the cockpit sill of his F-14B (BuNo 161422) after making an emergency arrested landing in Kuwait in September 2004. He recalled;

'We were flying over Iraq, north of Baghdad near Balad, on a routine XCAS mission when we lost our left engine. The oil system had a catastrophic failure and the engine seized up. We had the option to put her down right there in Balad, but the other engine and the hydraulics looked like they were holding up fine so we decided to try to make it back to Ali Al Salem, in Kuwait. It would have been impossible to replace the engine in Balad so it's a good thing that we made the decision we did' (*Lt(jg) Matt Koop*)

A VF-103 F-14B flies a mixed section patrol over Iraq with an F/A-18C of VFA-34 (*Lt(jg) Matt Koop*)

section and the helicopters were tasked with locating the blue van. We were told to contact a different JTAC who was actually in the town, and he duly gave us targeting information relating to where the van had last been seen. While I was working the FLIR in our LTS, my pilot was scouring the streets with his binoculars. We soon spotted an abandoned blue van, and the helicopters came in to confirm that this was indeed the insurgents' vehicle. With this confirmation, the Cobra was cleared to destroy the van with rockets.

'While the AH-1W was firing at the van, new reports were coming in and being passed to us on the radio that additional Marines had been engaged by insurgents who were holed up in a "café". The troops had been subjected to both machine gun fire and RPG rounds, and they were in need of immediate air support. This "café" was less than a kilometre from where we had found the van, and after a quick talk-on by the JTAC, we confirmed that we were "tally the target". He then requested that we provide laser designation for a Hellfire missile that was to be fired by the gunner in the Cobra, since his line-of-site for missile guidance was poor.

'Neither my pilot or I had ever done anything like this before, having never been briefed on how to lase for a Hellfire missile! But we had briefed on buddy lasing for our Hornet wingman's Laser Maverick, and we figured that the two laser-guided weapons were similar enough to expect success if we employed the same tactics. We were right. The Hellfire guided to the dead centre of our crosshairs and blew right through the front door of the building. That hit stopped the fire that our troops were receiving, but the weapon's small warhead caused minimal damage to the structure of the building itself.

'With the possibility of more insurgents hiding deeper in the "café", the order was given for us to destroy the building with our two GBU-12s. We were told to target each end of the building with one bomb, so we would have to make two passes with as little time in between as possible.

'As soon as we had received permission to drop our LGBs, we raced out to an appropriate run-in position which minimised the danger posed to our troops nearby. Fortunately, our LTS pod was producing a crisp image, and the target was easily identifiable from more than five miles

The pilot of VF-103's CAG jet (BuNo 162918) has extended the fighter's tailhook in preparation for landing back aboard CV-67 on 13 July 2004. The unit had only been on-station in the NAG for three days when this photograph was taken. Exactly one week later VF-103 dropped its first GBU-12 of the deployment on an insurgent position near Baghdad. A further 20 would be expended in anger by the unit over the next four-and-a-half months. On 5 January 2005, Lt(jg) Matt Koop was the RIO in BuNo 162918 when the fighter made its final flight from Oceana to AMARC, where it was placed in storage (*Lt(jg) Matt Koop*)

A VF-103 section breaks into the overhead above CV-67 on a typically hazy day in the NAG in August 2004, both jets returning home with their mission load-out of two GBU-12s apiece still intact (*Lt(jg) Matt Koop*)

away. We stepped through the checklist we had memorised and made sure that all our parameters were correct before dropping the first bomb. The weapon guided with perfect precision to the centre of my laser spot, destroying the east wing of the building. We immediately turned outbound and set up for our second run-in. This bomb came off just as well as the first, and it guided precisely to the target, levelling the structure.'

VF-103's support of Operation *Phantom Fury* lasted well into November, as the 1st MEF continued with its bloody campaign to rid the so-called 'Sunni Triangle' of insurgents. The unit persisted with flying mixed formations throughout this period, with the following account being related by a FAC(A)-qualified Tomcat pilot who was involved in just such a mission;

'Whilst leading a Hornet from VFA-83 on a routine *Phantom Fury* standby CAS mission in early November, with a second mixed section in-country with us, we were told to look at a building on the outskirts of Falluja. It was one of many targets we had received imagery and information for prior to launching, the second Navy section being told to investigate another dwelling nearby. Once both buildings were confirmed as being safe houses for insurgents, their destruction was approved. After locating our targets, we were told to deliver a single

1000-lb JDAM on each building. We carried LGBs on our Tomcats, so the JDAM-equipped Hornets would be primary strikers.

'We joined both sections together into a four-jet division so as to facilitate precise timings for the attack. Essentially, the F/A-18s joined as a lead section, with the F-14s in trail capturing BHA. This proved to be an ideal arrangement for us, as it made the best use of our LTS sensor, which turned out to be key to our successful attack.

'The Hornets' runs on the targets went well, with single bombs impacting each of the buildings virtually instantaneously. However, the JDAM from my Hornet wingman did not explode, or was a dud. Luckily, we could confirm this using LTS imagery in the cockpit, as both my RIO and I spotted the small puff of smoke on the roof of the building as the bomb hit home.

'We passed this information on to the decision makers on the ground, along with the fact that the building was still standing. I recommended a re-attack, and within minutes, we were authorised to expend our two 500-lb GBU-12s on the target. This we duly did with the minimum of fuss, scoring a direct hit. The size of the resulting explosion verified that not only had we hit the building, but also the JDAM inside. Surprisingly, given the fact that three bombs had now struck the building, most of the resulting damage was restricted to within the walls of the target itself – a testament to the accuracy of both the JDAM and the LGB.

'While this was not the most intense mission flown over Iraq during the course of our final Tomcat cruise, it provides a good illustration of the mixed section concept, and its strengths. Flying with the F/A-18s allowed CVW-17 to bring a more diverse range of weaponry to the fight. The Tomcat's sensors, employed by a dedicated operator in the form of the RIO, proved invaluable in target acquisition, allowing precision and flexibility in targeting, and keeping everyone honest as a BHA platform. Combine this with the jet's longer loitering time and the situational awareness of a second aircrew, and the F-14 became arguably the CAS platform of choice for operations in Iraq.'

CV-67 was relieved on station in the NAG by CVN-75 in late November 2004, by which time VF-103 had flown 384 OIF sorties totalling 1913.4 hours. The unit had also dropped 21 GBU-12s in anger whilst on-station.

As this book goes to press, CVN-75's CVW-3 is standing the OIF watch in the NAG, its trio of Hornet units again flying mixed formations with the ten F-14Bs of VF-32 – like VF-103, this unit is making its final Tomcat deployment. Unlike CVW-17, CVW-3 has not yet been called on to directly engage insurgents, although it continues to fly 'show of force' operations – including overseeing the Iraqi elections on 30 January 2005 – and convoy protection missions on a near daily basis.

Fittingly, the final chapter in the Tomcat's long career with the Navy will be played out in the NAG in the summer of 2005 when CVW-8, embarked in CVN-71, arrives on station to support OIF operations. Assigned to the air wing for this historic cruise will be VF-31 and VF-213, both of which will be conducting their final deployments with the F-14D prior to transitioning to Super Hornets in 2006. The final cat shot for the 'Last of the Big Fighters' is now just months away.

VF-32 returned to Iraqi skies in late November 2004, being tasked with conducting ISR and XCAS missions across the country from CVN-75. The latter sorties would see Navy jets providing on-call (alert) CAS, which meant that crews were a CAS asset for the period they were assigned to patrol over Iraq, but they were not allocated to a particular unit at the time that the ATO was written. As this book went to press, the unit has not yet been called on to drop ordnance in anger. Nevertheless, as this 9 February 2005 shot of 'Gypsy 100' (BuNo 162916) proves, every time a VF-32 jet ventures into Iraq it is armed with at least two GBU-12s. CVN-75 is scheduled to be relieved by CVN-70 in the NAG in late March 2005, thus bringing to an end the F-14B's operational service with Fifth Fleet. VF-32 is scheduled to have transitioned to the F/A-18F Super Hornet by early 2006 (*PH Ryan O'Connor*)

US NAVY F-14 TOMCAT UNITS INVOLVED IN OIF TO DATE

CVW-1 (USS *Enterprise* (CVN-65)) in OIF II

VF-211 'FIGHTING CHECKMATES' (F-14A)

161612/100	161603/101	162610/102	158632/103
158635/104	161626/105	158628/110	161295/111*
161275/114	161297/115		

* declared written-off following mid-air collision over Red Sea with BuNo 158635 on 2 February 2004. Both jets landed safely aboard CVN-65

CVW-2 (USS *Constellation* (CV-64)) in OIF I

VF-2 'BOUNTY HUNTERS' (F-14D)

163894/100	159630/101	164346/102	164350/103
163900/104	163418/105	164342/106	159595/107
164345/110	159613/111		

CVW-3 (USS *Harry S Truman* (CVN-75)) in OIF I

VF-32 'SWORDSMEN' (F-14B)

162916/100	161860/101	162915/103	163410/104
163216/105	163224/107	162703/110	161428/111
161608/112	161424/114		

CVW-3 (USS *Harry S Truman* (CVN-75)) in OIF III

VF-32 'SWORDSMEN' (F-14B)

162916/100	161860/101	162692/102	162915/103
163410/104	163216/105	163224/107	162703/110
161428/111	161424/114		

CVW-5 (USS *Kitty Hawk* (CV-63)) in OIF I

VF-154 'BLACK KNIGHTS' (F-14A)

161866/100	161276/101	161280/102	161293/103
158620/104*/**	161271/105	161291/106	161296/107*
161288/110*	161292/111*	158624/112*	162697/113

* shore-based at Al Udeid, Qatar, during OIF
** crashed in Iraq on 2/4/03 due to engine failure

CVW-7 (USS *George Washington* (CVN-73)) in OIF II

VF-11 'RED RIPPERS' (F-14B)

163227/200	162912/201	161418/202	163408/203
163218/204	162927/205	162925/206	162911/210
162919/211	163409/212		

VF-143 'PUKIN' DOGS' (F-14B)

163220/100	163407/101	162921/102	161421/103
162926/105	161434/106	161441/110	162701/111
161870/112	162924/114		

CVW-8 (USS *Theodore Roosevelt* (CVN-71)) in OIF I

VF-213 'BLACK LIONS' (F-14D)

164602/100	164341/101	163896/102	163899/103
159628/104	161163/105	163893/106	161166/107
163903/110	159629/111		

CVW-14 (USS *Abraham Lincoln* (CVN-72)) in OIF I

VF-31 'TOMCATTERS' (F-14D)

164601/100	164600/101	163904/102	164344/103
163898/104	159610/105	164343/106	163413/107
159618/110	163895/111		

CVW-17 (USS *John F Kennedy* (CV-67)) in OIF III

VF-103 'JOLLY ROGERS' (F-14B)

162918/100	162705/101	161419/102	163217/103
161442/104	163229/105	161862/107	161435/110
162695/111	161422/112		

COLOUR PLATES

1
F-14D BuNo 163894 of VF-2, USS *Constellation* (CV-64), Pacific Ocean, May 2003
See page 52 for the jet's airframe/OIF history.

2
F-14D BuNo 164342 of VF-2, USS *Constellation* (CV-64), NAG, April 2003
'Bullet 106' was the first VF-2 jet to fire its 20 mm cannon in anger during OIF (see page 64 for details). A prolific bomber during the campaign, it finished second only to VF-2's CAG jet in terms of the number of LGBs (46) and JDAM (five) it expended. Delivered new to VF-124 on 22 August 1991, this aircraft served with VF-31 and VF-101 (including the unit's Miramar det) until transferred to VF-2 in 2000. BuNo 164342 returned to VF-101 following VF-2's switch to the F/A-18F in mid-2003.

3
F-14D BuNo 164601 of VF-31, USS *Abraham Lincoln* (CVN-72), NAG, April 2003
VF-31's CAG jet dropped 19 JDAM/LGBs in OIF. See page 27 for the jet's airframe/OIF history.

4
F-14D BuNo 164600 of VF-31, USS *Abraham Lincoln* (CVN-72), NAG, April 2003
Configured for TARPS, and therefore never fitted with an LTS pod, 'Tomcatter 101' dropped just 11 bombs in OIF. The aircraft also had its tail markings changed towards the end of VF-31's marathon ten-month CVN-72 deployment, its famous 'Felix and the bomb' motif being moved from the fins to just forward of the engine intakes in place of the star and bar. The small CVW-14 NK code was also drastically enlarged to cover the entire fin. See scrap view 4 for details. An airframe and OIF history for this jet appears on page 7.

5
F-14D BuNo 159610 of VF-31, USS *Abraham Lincoln* (CVN-72), NAG, April 2003
VF-31's oldest jet, 'Tomcatter 105' had the unique distinction of not dropping a single bomb in OIF! The designated 'hangar queen', it remained below decks aboard CVN-72 and acted as a 'parts tree' for the remaining nine jets in the unit. By the time it flew off *Lincoln* to Oceana on 30 April 2003, it had been adorned with a unique 'service medal' that bore the inscription *I GAVE SO OTHERS COULD FLY* – see scrap view 5 for details. Delivered to the Navy in August 1975, the aircraft's service highlight came on 4 January 1989 when it was one of two VF-32 Tomcats to down a pair Libyan MiG-23 'Flogger-Es' over the Gulf of Sidra. Converted into an F-14D the following year, the jet served almost exclusively with VF-31 up until it was stricken by the unit on 31 May 2003. The jet has been on display in the Steven F Udvar Hazy Center at Dulles Airport since 14 November 2003.

6
F-14A BuNo 161276 of VF-154, USS *Kitty Hawk* (CV-63), NAG, April 2003
VF-154 adorned both its CAG and CO jets in identical markings. Flying exclusively from *Kitty Hawk*, 'Nite 101' dropped 45 LGBs in OIF – a tally second only to 'Nite 103', which expended 51 LGBs. Delivered new to VF-2 on 25 June 1981, the jet spent the next 15 years flying with Miramar-based units including VF-213. It moved to Oceana when the Navy handed 'Fightertown' over to the Marine Corps in 1996, joining VF-211. BuNo 161276 was sent to NAF Atsugi on 15 December 1999 to join VF-154, and the 'Black Knights' duly marked it up as the CO's aircraft. The fighter served as 'Nite 101' until flown back to Oceana with the unit in September 2003, where it was stricken on 16 December that same year.

7
F-14A BuNo 161296 of VF-154, USS *Kitty Hawk* (CV-63), NAG, April 2003
'Nite 107' was one of five VF-154 jets to fly from Al Udeid air base for much of OIF. The Tomcat dropped 32 LGBs during the war, and was also unique in being the only 'Black Knight' F-14 to fire its Vulcan cannon in anger – note the gun emblem forward of the bomb tally. Delivered new to VF-1 on 6 March 1982, the aircraft subsequently saw fleet service with VF-21, VF-114, VF-2 and VF-124 at Miramar, followed by VF-32 at Oceana from 1995. Placed in storage at NAS Jacksonville in late 1996, BuNo 161296 was transferred to VF-41 in 2000 and saw combat in OSW and OEF during CVW-8's 2001 deployment aboard CVN-65. VF-41 transitioned onto the F/A-18F upon its return home, and BuNo 161296 was passed to VF-154 on 12 January 2002. The jet came back to Oceana with the unit in September 2003 and was stricken by year-end.

8
F-14B BuNo 162916 of VF-32, USS *Harry S Truman* (CVN-75), Mediterranean Sea, April 2003
Delivered new to VF-143 in April 1988, the fighter joined VF-103 in 1994 and then VF-102 in early 1997. It served as the latter unit's CAG jet until transferred to VF-32 three years later to fill a similar role. Marked in full squadron colours, BuNo 162916 saw combat over Iraq during *Truman's* maiden deployment in 2000-01, and then again in OIF. In the latter conflict it flew 28 missions totalling 131.3 combat hours, and expended 29 GBU-12s, one GBU-16 and five GBU-31. Aside from its mission markings, the aircraft also featured the old CVW-3 emblem on the inside of its twin fins (see scrap view 8 for details). This jet is presently deployed in the NAG.

9
F-14B BuNo 161860 of VF-32, USS *Harry S Truman* (CVN-75), Mediterranean Sea, April 2003
'Gypsy 101' was marked with the new CVW-3

badge on the inside of its fins (see scrap view 9). See page 78 for the jet's airframe/OIF history.

10
F-14B BuNo 163224 of VF-32, USS *Harry S Truman* (CVN-75), Mediterranean Sea, April 2003
Bearing the Modex 107, this aircraft was the natural choice to be marked up in honour of NASA crew STS-107 who perished when Space Shuttle *Columbia* broke up upon re-entry on 1 February 2003. BuNo 163224 flew 35 missions totalling 144.5 hours during OIF, dropping 23 GBU-12s, six GBU-16s and 14 GBU-31s. Delivered new to VF-24 in June 1989, this jet spent time with VF-142, VF-101, VF-102 and VF-103, before joining VF-32 in late 1999. It is still serving with the unit today.

11
F-14D BuNo 164602 of VF-213, USS *Theodore Roosevelt* (CVN-71), Mediterranean Sea, April 2003
'Blacklion 100' dropped the most ordnance (31 JDAM/LGBs) of any VF-213 jet in OIF, the aircraft also featuring a *HIGH NOON* 'six-shooter' emblem beneath its front cockpit. This award was given to the Navy fighter squadron that achieved the best scores in aerial gunnery in an annual contest held at Oceana. This jet saw combat with VF-213 in 1998, and again with the unit in OEF in 2001-02. BuNo 164602 was delivered new to VF-124 on 14 August 1992 and transferred to VF-2 in late 1994. When VF-213 swapped its F-14As for D-models in late 1997, BuNo 164602 was one of the jets it received from VF-2. The aircraft has remained with VF-213 ever since.

12
F-14D BuNo 163893 of VF-213, USS *Theodore Roosevelt* (CVN-71), Mediterranean Sea, April 2003
Aside from being the *High Noon* winners, VF-213 had also received the Admiral Joseph Clifton award in 2002 as the best fighter unit in the Navy. And to top it off, the 'Black Lions' had also received the Golden Wrench award for the best jet availability rates in CVW-8, a Battle E for sustained combat efficiency and a Safety S. Markings denoting these awards were worn on the tails of all VF-213 jets in 2003. BuNo 163893 also had an OEF silhouette in the shape of Afghanistan applied beneath the rear cockpit, onto which was stencilled the number 70 for the number of bombs it had dropped in the conflict. Expending a further 23 JDAM/LGBs in OIF, BuNo 163893 had also seen combat in *Desert Fox*. Delivered new to VF-124 on 31 August 1990, the aircraft served with VF-101 Det A (from 1994) and VF-31 (from September 1995), before joining VF-213 in late 1997.

13
F-14A BuNo 161603 of VF-211, USS *Enterprise* (CVN-65), NAG, January 2004
VF-211's CO jet was a riot of colour during the unit's final Tomcat deployment, this aircraft being marked with *Clifton* and *GRAND SLAM PRECISION STRIKE AWARD* titling, a Battle E and a Safety S.

Delivered new to VF-124 on 1 July 1983, the aircraft later served with VF-21, VF-2, VF-24 and VF-213. Placed in storage in the late 1990s, BuNo 161603 joined VF-14 in early 2001 and saw combat in OSW and OEF. It was passed on to VF-211 in early 2002 when VF-14 commenced its conversion onto the F/A-18E, and the jet remained with the latter unit until flown to AMARC in October 2004.

14
F-14B BuNo 161418 of VF-11, USS *George Washington* (CVN-73), NAG, April 2004
VF-11 marked all of its F-14s with AIM-54-inspired nose art during its NAG deployment, thus denoting its status as the last Navy unit (along with sister-squadron VF-143) to take the Phoenix missile to sea. Both of CVW-7's Tomcat squadrons made MissilEx history within days of arriving in the NAG when, on 25 February 2005, both units fired eight AIM-54s apiece. Delivered new to VF-101 on 21 May 1982, this aircraft became the fourth F-14B upgrade in 1988 and subsequently served with VF-74, VF-143, VF-142, VF-101 and VF-103. It has been assigned to VF-11 since 1999.

15
F-14B BuNo 162926 of VF-143, USS *George Washington* (CVN-73), NAG, April 2004
Delivered new to VF-103 in November 1988, and seeing action in *Desert Storm* with the unit, this aircraft later served with VF-142, VF-143 and VF-32, before rejoining VF-143 once again in late 1998.

16
F-14B BuNo 162918 of VF-103, USS *John F Kennedy* (CV-67), NAG, November 2004
VF-103's CAG jet dropped two LGBs during the unit's 2004 NAG deployment. Delivered new to VF-102 in July 1988, it joined VF-101 eight years later and VF-103 in 2000. The aircraft was retired to AMARC on 5 January 2005.

17
F-14B BuNo 163217 of VF-103, USS *John F Kennedy* (CV-67), NAG, November 2004
VF-103's CO jet has always been Modex 103 for obvious reasons. The most colourful F-14 in the squadron, BuNo 163217 dropped four LGBs whilst in the NAG in 2004. The fighter had been delivered new to VF-142 in January 1989, after which it served with VF-143. Joining VF-103 in 1998, the jet was transferred to VF-102 two years later. Seeing combat in CVW-1's 2001-02 OEF cruise, the F-14 was assigned to VF-101 in 2002 and then VF-103 in 2003. It too went to AMARC in January 2005.

18
F-14B BuNo 161435 of VF-103, USS *John F Kennedy* (CV-67), NAG, November 2004
A *Desert Storm* veteran with VF-74, this jet served exclusively with VF-103 following its arrival from VF-102 in 1998. The F-14B expended three LGBs during VF-103's final Tomcat deployment in 2004.